SHIPWRECKS
AND *LEGENDS*
'ROUND CAPE MAY

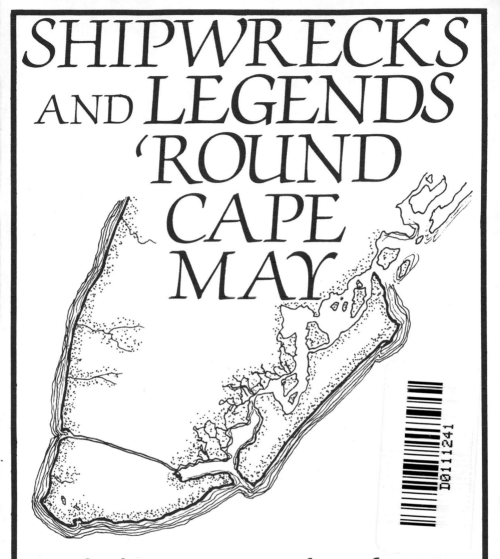

Includes Stirring Tales Of.....
·PIRATES ·BURIED TREASURE
·RUM-RUNNERS ·WAR ACTION
....plus 20 Pages Of Photos!

David J. Seibold   Charles J. Adams III

SHIPWRECKS AND LEGENDS 'ROUND CAPE MAY
by David J. Seibold and Charles J. Adams III

Copyright 1987

For information, write to:
Exeter House Books
P.O. Box 8134
Reading, PA 19603

ISBN: 0-9610008-5-6

PRINTED IN THE UNITED STATES OF AMERICA

TABLE OF CONTENTS

INTRODUCTION

Quite a place, this Cape May. America's first resort town, with its Victorian homes and hostelries of gaudy pastels and lacy woodwork, is a happy summer place where happy summer people frolic in the sand, shops and streets of this festive area.

But when the pages of time are turned back, or when the summer sun sets, this is a cape of mystery, intrigue and rich folklore.

What you are reading does not pretend to masquerade as a history book. While carefully conceived, planned, and despite exhaustive research and intensive interviews, this is only an overview of Cape May's most noteworthy legends and shipwrecks.

At times, there may seem to be more questions than answers for some of these tales. The complete stories are often so elusive and lost in time, and information so contradictory, that any iron-clad conclusions are precluded.

Just how may "privateers," for example, sailed from Cape May? How many Spanish, French and Colonial ships taunted British ships off the cape during the Revolution? The simple definition of "privateer" versus "pirate" is made complex due to contemporary interpretation and historical acceptance.

The entrance to the Delaware Bay, the maritime approach to Philadelphia, has always been strategic. Dozens of Cape May residents are listed as those who participated in Revolutionary War and War of 1812 bay defenses. Some were on scows armed with small cannons, others were on ships disguised as merchantmen or fishing vessels that turned into fighters when British sails were sighted.

There were sea battles in the bay, there were blockades of the bay, and there was mining of the bay. From the Revolution to World War II, Cape May was close to the front of the wars at sea.

This fact has left Cape May with its legends, its relics and its scars of war. Coastal watch towers still exist on Cape May, grim reminders of how close World War II came to the cape. Tragically, many visitors to the area may not even know (or care) what they were. One of the towers is today girdled by the Queen's Inn, on the oceanfront in Cape May. It was last used in the 1970s for radar calibrations, but is now used for storage by humans and for roosting by pigeons.

There are other relics. The relentless sea at Cape May Point is claiming more of the massive 1942 gun bunker every year, but it remains as another reminder of the war at the shore.

Some reminders are not tangible. Rumors and stories continue to be told about the German spies who landed on Cape May and became a part of everyday society here, while somehow relaying vital information back to the U-boats that ventured within sight of the Cape May beaches.

There is a persistent story of the Nazi sub captured just off the cape, brought into an American port intact and found to have a day-old copy of the Philadelphia Bulletin newspaper and a fresh loaf of Bond bread in "der Kapitan's" cabin.

Not all of the most confounding and fascinating tales of Cape May involve times of war. Lake Lily (or Lily Lake, or Lily Pond, as it has been called by various accounts at various times) is a legendary little body of water near Cape May Point.

It is said that British warships in two wars replenished their freshwater supply with water from the lake. When the local freedom fighters learned of it, they dug a trench from sea to lake and fouled the clear water to ruin the British plans.

At Cape May Point, of course, is the Cape May Light, which itself harbors a legend or two. The present 145-foot tower was built in 1859, and replaced other lighthouses that existed there since 1822.

There are old stories of older, wooden lighthouses at the point. There has been some speculation, believed to be false by serious Cape May historians, that the first lighthouse was built there as early as the 1740s.

In any event, the presence of the lighthouse, off-shore light ships, Life-Saving Stations and later Coast Guard bases on Cape May has added to the strong nautical flavor of Cape May.

That flavor is spiced by more speculative and chilling legends—legends that include images of monsters, pirates and ghosts.

What's more, some of Cape May's alleged spectres step right out of the pages of history books.

Captain Kidd, alas and admittedly, probably never buried any treasure on Cape May. But is there something wrong with perpetuating the legend that he just might have? Who of us can know for certain?

There are vague references to Kidd's landing here, and it is even inferred that his dastardly crews partook of Lake Lily's fresh water. Until the early 1890s, a tree stood near the Cape May Point Light, and it was beneath that tree that the pirate was said to have rested for a time.

Those who keep the fires of folk tales burning say the ghosts of Captain Kidd or perhaps Blackbeard still find time in their eternal sojourn to walk the beaches of Cape May. Indeed, in their book, "The Jersey Devil," authors James F. McCloy and Ray Miller Jr. say that the headless ghost of one of Kidd's crewmen, stationed in death to guard buried treasure somewhere on the New Jersey shore, is out there somewhere. The ghost, which haunted the beaches in solitary for many years, reportedly even met the Jersey Devil and the two malevolent, kindred spirits teamed up to double the horror for unsuspecting mortals who happened to cross their path.

This, of course, is the stuff of fiction and fantasy. Captain Kidd was probably never here. The Jersey Devil never existed. Ghosts aren't real. Or was he, did it, and are they? Who of us can know for certain?

The ghost of a young woman doesn't really pace from the dunes to the Cape May Point Light under full moons. The spirit of a restless former resident doesn't really haunt the stately home near Rio Grande. There never was a day-old Philadelphia bulletin found inside a captured German sub.

Or does she? Does it? Was it?

Who of us can know for certain?

Hopefully, you are reading this book while spending a nice day or peaceful evening "down the shore" on Cape May. Read one of the accounts of a dramatic shipwreck just off shore and have a look out there at the horizon and imagine the drama.

Read about just how close the Germans brought their unterseeboots to Cape May and look to sea. Just this side of the horizon was once the most savage and threatening enemy this country ever faced. Stand atop the concrete bunker of Cape May Point and absorb its meaning and its place in history.

As for the pirates, the monsters and the ghosts—well, they never really existed, did they? But read about their legends anyway. And then, on the next foggy night, have a walk on the beach. Listen for the moans that are probably just distant animal sounds or the sound of the wind rustling through snowfences or dune grass. Follow with your eyes that glow just ahead of you that seems to be real, but probably is just an illusion. Feel the icy chill and fight the shivers, but remind yourself that although it is summertime, the sudden wisp of cold is just the ocean breeze.

None of it is real. It's all in your imagination.

Or is it?

None of us can know for certain.

A SEAFARING HERITAGE

To the millions of tourists and vacationers who know Cape May only as a charming Victorian town or a land of pleasant beaches, there is much to be learned.

While this volume does not in any way pretend to be an historical treatise, some background on the discovery, growth and development of the cape should be provided.

It should also be remembered that throughout this book, reference to "Cape May" is made in a very general, and yet very specific fashion.

As a popular retreat for daytrippers and resort for more long-term visitors, it is sometimes forgotten that this land is, after all, a cape. It is swept by the sometimes gentle, sometimes savage sea, and washed by the more docile bay. It is ravaged and romanced by the ocean, and that ocean has played an uncompromising and inextricable role in Cape May's history.

For the authors' purposes, Cape May is the thumb-shaped peninsula that pokes south from 39 degrees, 10 minutes latitude, roughly from Dennis Creek on the bay and from Ludlam Beach on the ocean front.

It is within these bounds that, some say, Henry Hudson and Giovanni Verazzano made landfall in the late sixteenth and early seventeenth centuries. It is there that, most certainly, Cornelius Mey, the Dutchman, came at about the same time the Mayflower was finding Cape Cod.

The earliest settlers on Cape May found sheltered, hospitable land on sandy bluffs. They also found, according to weathered and pitifully meager records, an abundance of whales just off shore.

1

Thus, whaling became the first "industry" and lure for those who made the cape their new home.

It is generally regarded that the first settlement of the white man on Cape May was at a rough-hewn village known variously as New England Town, Portsmouth and later, Town Bank. Located on the bay side of the cape, the tiny collection of crude shacks, boat houses and more substantial homes, Town Bank from the 1680s to the turn of the next century was home for those who harvested the bounty of the land during the spring and summer growing seasons and who then harvested the fruits of the bay and ocean in the short late-winter whaling season.

What early records do exist reveal settlers with names like Corson, Townsend and Schellinger—names that still today linger on maps and charts, and in the minds of all who take to the sea from Cape May.

The spirited hunt for the whales off Cape May pushed the massive sea beasts farther out to sea. Within a precious few years, the whalers' prey became elusive and the whaling of Cape May ran its course.

Town Bank, threatened even during its short, tenuous existence by persistent bay surf, was all but abandoned. One by one, the cabins and boat houses were claimed by encroaching waters, and what was Cape May's first white settlement is now but a memory, buried in the sand somewhere under the Delaware Bay.

THE PIRATES AT CAPE MAY

As the word of the burgeoning prosperity on the shores of Cape May spread, those who sought to take their share of it set sail for this intriguing and promising land. Some came with legitimate and honest ambitions, but others came in hopes of make a very fast, but very dishonest profit.

During the glory years of piracy, roughly from 1675 to 1725, history shows that several pirates set foot on Cape May area soil, and it is entirely possible that even more than what history records have landed there to resupply and repair their vessels, and perhaps . . . just perhaps . . . hide treasure!

James Logan, secretary of Pennsylvania colony, once estimated that there were no fewer than 1,500 pirates operating off the North American coast during the height of the period. It is true that many of these "pirates" were really privateers, that is, a ship and crew sanctioned by the British government to prey on any vessels belonging to governments not friendly with the British.

Still, piracy in the skull-and-crossbones, yo-ho-ho manner (or as close to it as it ever really came) was in its hey-day off Cape May.

CAPTAIN KIDD AT CAPE MAY?

One of the most famous and feared pirates that legend says buried treasure near Cape May is the notorious Captain William Kidd. To this day, the almost universal question remains: Where, if ever and anywhere, is Kidd's treasure buried?

In order to answer that question or even speculate on it, we must separate Capt. Kidd as history records from Capt. Kidd as folklore whispers.

Scottish by birth, Kidd came to America and apparently established a tranquil lifestyle in lower Manhattan. It is said that he owned a small home on what is now Wall Street, and even worshipped at Trinity Church nearby.

Most historians now believe Kidd was not a pirate, but actually a privateer. Kidd was not an evil, shrewd, cruel, marauding master of his ship and men, although he did kill a crew member while supressing a mutiny. Kidd was not even a successful plunderer of treasure-laden ships. In fact, only one vessel captured by Kidd, the "Quedagh Merchant," was loaded with any worthwhile treasure, in the romantic sense of the word.

There was a portion of what was believed to be "Captain Kidd's Treasure" buried on an island owned by a friend of Kidd's off the coast of eastern Long Island. A portion of it was subsequently discovered. Still, some of the booty from the Quedah Merchant has never been accounted for, and not for lack of trying.

Although some historians say there is no Kidd treasure to be found, anywhere, systematic and sometimes frenzied searches continue up and down the Atlantic coast.

The prize recovered on Gardiner's Island was supposedly retrieved by Kidd's friend, John Gardiner. Ironically, some of that treasure was sent to the governor of Massachusetts, who arrested him and charged him with crimes against the crown.

Even today, treasure hunters search Gardiner's Island for more loot. On Oak Island, Nova Scotia, the storied "Money Pit" has been the site of serious and expensive excavations for decades. Millions of dollars and man-hours of labor have been spent in a sometimes sophisticated-sometimes foolhardy quest for Kidd's treasure, although it is widely accepted and almost certain that Kidd never once set foot on Oak Island. Lives have been lost at the Money Pit, and the island has become a tourist attraction. It is said that Kidd's ghost even walks the dunes and hillocks of the little island in Mahone Bay.

Despite all historical protestations, the legend of Kidd and his treasure remains strong. There is even a belief that some of the ill-gotten fortune lies deep under the soil of Cape May.

On his way back to Boston from the East African coast, Kidd lingered in the West Indies with the captured vessel, Quedah Merchant and his prize of silks, emeralds, silver, gold, sugar, iron, muslin and weapons, totalling some $100,000.

While in harbor, Kidd found out that there was a bounty out for his arrest as a pirate. Upon first hearing of it, he was visibly shaken. "There must be some mistake," he is said to have bellowed. "I'm a privateer, not a pirate."

At that moment, Kidd's crew wanted to disband, but the determined captain wanted to go to America to correct the "mistake."

Kidd abandoned the toredo worm-damaged hulk of the Quedah Merchant and purchased, with a portion of the purloined prizes, another vessel called the "Antonio."

Kidd, now 50 years old, wanted to go back and live out his life with his family. Aboard the Antonio, he sailed again to New York.

Legend has it that Kidd was well aware that he better hide some of his captured cargo before sailing into New York Harbor. One of Kidd's hiding places, according to that legend, was Cape May. The treasure, so goes the story, was deposited somewhere on the cape, and just as soon as Kidd got the piracy mess straightened out, he would return and reclaim the loot.

Kidd was thrown in jail, and two years later convicted of piracy in an English court. Most historians now admit that the deck was stacked against Kidd, and the trial was a cruel joke. Kidd wasn't even permitted counsel for his defense. The government, apparently, was out to use Kidd as an example of what would happen to a captured pirate.

On May 23, 1701, in the disgusting section of London known as Wapping, Kidd was hanged on Execution Dock. "This is a very fickle and faithless generation," Kidd said in exasperation as they tightened the noose around his neck. "I am the most innocent of all."

The legend continues that there is still treasure hidden somewhere, and perhaps on Cape May. At his trial, Kidd boasted that he could quickly and easily come up with 100,000 pounds with which to defend himself or buy his freedom. While in a London jail cell, Kidd also wrote to Massachusetts governor Lord Bellemont, that he could dig up 50 pounds of gold for favors in his trial.

For the purposes of this book, it is worth noting that following Kidd's execution, all but one member of his convicted crew were released. Two of those crewmen came to South Jersey to settle.

Could it be that they returned because they knew that some of Captain Kidd's treasure indeed was buried here?

In the next chapter, we shall discuss this question in more detail, and also talk with modern-day treasure hunters who have their own thoughts on the alleged Kidd treasure, and insight into even more reported treasure ships on the shores of Cape May.

First, though, let us examine some of the other pirates who have operated in the waters off the cape, in fact or in legend.

BLACKBEARD

His name was either Edward Teach, Edward Thatch, or perhaps even Edward Drummond. To the world, however, he was the most ruthless pirate of them all. So ruthless was he, that it is said he made a captor eat his own ears and nose before he was killed!

Blackbeard, as he was known, is only afforded a cursory mention in the annals of Cape May's history. It is widely accepted that he did sail past the cape, up the bay and river to Philadelphia with plans to see the busy port, but after he discovered that there was a "dead or alive" warrant out on him, he left with great haste and returned to more familiar territory along the Carolinas.

While it is doubtful that Blackbeard ever landed on Cape May, some believe he buried a portion of his treasure in Delaware, along what became known as Blackbird (a corruption of the pirate's name?) Creek. Others think more than ten tons of Blackbird's booty is deposited on the New Jersey side of the bay near Villas, or even far upstream at Burlington, where in 1926 some digging was done in hopes of finding the cache.

Captains Kidd and Blackbeard are both mentioned in popular Cape May legends that suggest both, in their times, landed at the tip of the cape and went to Lake Lilly (a.k.a. Lilly Pond) for fresh water. That lake figures in another legend of the time local patriots dug a channel from the sea to the freshwater lake when they discovered the British crews were tapping the lake to fill their casks during the Revolution. The salt water seeped into the fresh, thus foiling the Redcoats' plans and fouling their drinking water.

GILES SHELLEY

This lesser known pirate did, it is generally believed, set foot on Cape May. While not as notorious as Kidd or Blackbeard, Shelley was their equal, and his name was mentioned in the Kidd trials in London.

Like Kidd, with whom Shelley once sailed, it could be said that Shelley was more a privateer than a pirate. And like Kidd, Shelley was a wanted man in South Jersey. Records in the Cape May County Sheriff's Department indicate that the county's first sheriff was actually put on alert that Kidd was in his area. Later, the governor of East and West Jersey, Jeremiah Basse, issued an arrest warrant for Shelley and sent a force to intercept the pirate's ship, "Nassau."

This force manned a sloop and was successful in capturing four of Shelley's men and chests full of plundered gold, silver, amber and silk.

The four captured men were committed to the Burlington jail, but Shelley was not among them.

Shelley was known to have come in and out of the inlets around Cape May, taking on and dropping off men as his crews changed. One of those men was a Dr. Robert Bradinham, who was William Kidd's physician. The good doctor was one former Kidd compatriate who turned king's evidence and helped in the conviction of Captain Kidd.

There could be speculation that because Giles Shelley seemed to use Cape May as a way station, it would follow that he used it also as a depository for any treasure that needed to be stashed.

RICHARD WORLEY

Here was short-time, small-time pirate who was, for a spell, the scourge of the Delaware Bay. His reign lasted only about three months.

The lure of the exciting life of piracy excited Worley. Being an impetuous man, he turned his small fishing boat into a pirate ship and his ten crewmen into instant corsairs. He robbed every small fishing vessel and coaster he could intercept, and grew bolder with each success, no matter how small it was.

In a daring move, Worley's crew managed to capture a much larger vessel off Cape May in 1718. As the word of his latest feat hit the ports along the bay, Worley and his ten men in their small fishing craft became exaggerated to scores of cutthroats in a sleek ship with all the modern cannon and equipment of the day.

In reality, Worley was still a bush-leaguer. His booty was usually small casks of rum, a few pieces of gold and silver, and assorted weapons and personal items.

After the capture of the larger sloop just off Cape May, and the notoriety it received, Worley apparently decided he was ready for the major leagues of piracy. He set sail for Florida and perhaps the Bahamas in search of the "big hit."

Worley's luck was running out. Off the coast of the Carolinas there was an all-out search for the wicked Blackbeard. The unsuspecting Worley found himself caught in a trap set for Blackbeard.

A sea battle ensued, and Worley and his crew were killed by colonial authorities. Again, the episode was aggrandized and by the time word reached the shore, what was an unspectacular skirmish had turned into a swashbuckling exploit. In town, it was learned that "a pirate had been killed" in the melee. The towns-folk rejoiced, thinking it was the end of Blackbeard and his terror.

But Blackbeard it was not. It was only Richard Worley, the hapless Delaware Bay fisherman-turned-pirate, who met his end just weeks after hoisting his Jolly Roger!

STEDE BONNET

Known as the "Gentleman Pirate," Bonnet was thought to be basically a man of honor, a man of liberal education, and a former gentleman planter.

In fact, it was a wonder as to why Stede Bonnet got involved with piracy in the first place, since at one time he was a respected citizen. A former army major and Barbados plantation owner, Bonnet took to the sea for what could be called a very basic reason.

Historians believe he simply wasn't happy at home. It has been stated in many contemporary references that Bonnet's wife was an overbearing, obnoxious nag. He turned to piracy to get away from his wife!

Bonnet's Cape May connection is the capture of the sloop "Francis." The victim was anchored at the mouth of the Delaware Bay, about eight miles out. Bonnet and some his crewmen waited until evening, rowed a small boat to the side of the Francis and boarded her. All aboard the sloop were taken by surprise, but living up to his reputation, Bonnet promised not to harm any of the Francis' crew if they promised in turn not to resist. The tale is told of how Bonnet's pirates and the Francis' crew drank rum together while the sloop was ravished of its wealth and cargo. Bonnet thanked his captives and went on to another challenge.

Later in his career, Bonnet joined forces with Blackbeard, in an unlikely pairing of a renowned murderer and a more placid plunderer.

Somehow, Bonnet was credited with the practice of forcing uncooperative victims to "walk the plank." Actually, most historians who rely on written fact for proof cannot find evidence to support this claim. Pirates were cruel in many cases, and undoubtedly Bonnet overstepped his "gentlemanly" reputation to

9

indulge in some of that cruelty, but walking a plank to certain death at sea was never substantiated.

Stede Bonnet was captured in a fierce sea battle off the coast of the Carolinas, just before Richard Worley was slain. Soon after being taken, Bonnet managed to escape, only to be re-captured in short order. He was later found guilty of piracy and executed. Even on his way to meet his maker, he remained the consummate gentleman. He was hanged while cradling a nose-gay in his cupped hands.

SAMUEL BELLAMY

This man was the "orator pirate." He was probably one of the more successful pirates in terms of wealth accumulated through pillaging on the high seas.

Although known in some accounts as "Charles" Bellamy, it is thought that the man's name actually was Samuel, and "Black Sam" he is in folklore.

His bold declarations and boasting eventually became his downfall. Once, he put the word out that he was leaving the Caribbean hunting grounds he picked clean. He would head north, he said, to Cape May. He would wreak havoc with the plentiful shipping between Philadelphia and New York and re-plenish his ship's supply of food, ammunition and petty luxuries. After loading up, he continued, he would continue up the coast to Nova Scotia, where he could take advantage of the tides and clean the bottom of their vessel, the "Whydah."

Black Sam and his heavies preyed on Delaware Bay mer-chantmen for a period, and after fulfilling his plans, Bellamy headed to Nova Scotia.

The celebration aboard the Whydah apparently got out of hand. The crew became uncontrollably drunk, a rough storm came up, and the pirates were swept onto the beach near what is now Wellfleet, Cape Cod. In their inebriated state, the crewmen were easily captured by local authorities and bounty hunters aware of the Whydah's northern trek. They stood trial, and were hanged.

It is entirely possible that Black Sam Bellamy could have deposited some of his loot somewhere on Cape May while he plied nearby waters. Nobody could know for certain.

Barry Clifford, a Massachusetts salvor, believes he knows for certain that Black Sam's ship is buried about 25 feet in the sand in the Cape Cod surf.

Clifford discovered the remains of the Whydah in 1982, and is actively pursuing its salvage and a possible "Black Sam" pirate museum nearby. The discovery represents the first time a pirate's vessel has ever been discovered, and someday what is left of the ship and its cargo, which beached in 1717, may again see the light of day.

MOONCUSSERS

Almost certainly, the coasts of Cape May could not have escaped the wrath of the wreckers—the dreaded "mooncussers" who found easy pickings on dark nights along the New Jersey shore.

They cussed the moon because its bright light exposed them to the ships they hoped to lure onto the shoals and beaches.

These shorebound pirates were known to walk along the beach on moonless nights with a lantern strapped to a horse or mule. The light in the distance would appear to be the light on a ship, and helmsmen on vessels sailing close-in felt secure that they could hug the shore even closer since there were other lights on other boats closer to the beach.

Not knowing the lights were actually on the beach, the helmsman brought his vessel closer, only to run aground. The band of mooncussers, also known as "wreckers," scurried out to the helpless ship and salvaged (stole) what they could.

The "Gravely Run Pirates" are perhaps the best known of the local mooncussers, but not much more than their name and technique remains.

Any heritage with a folklore spiced with names like Captain Kidd, Blackbeard and the like is worth holding on to and cherishing. Did any of these legendary pirates really walk the beaches of Cape May? Who can say for sure?

Every once in a while, ancient gold and silver is found somewhere near or on the cape. Every once in a while, another "dig" for "pirate's treasure" commences. In April, 1922, residents of Cape May organized to try to recover what was believed to be $5 million worth of gold aboard the wreckage of a "Spanish vessel" that was partially visible on the northern tip of Two-Mile Beach. Later in the century, another report reached the press that a researcher confirmed that a portion of Jean Lafitte's treasure was secreted somewhere on the rim of the Delaware Bay by Dominique You, brother of the legendary Louisiana pirate merchant.

Such stories are not confined to the dark long-ago. Humanity must have its heroes and its villains. Despite whatever was real, and whatever was the truth, and whatever was blown totally out of proportion, men like Kidd, Teach, Bellamy and Worley have become the villains of the sea.

Their alleged acts continue to fascinate people, even in the enlightened and sophisticated late twentieth century. Their memories continue to inspire men to write books, read those books, and sometimes even risk life and personal fortunes to seek the mysteries of other lives and perhaps larger fortunes.

IN SEARCH OF CAPE MAY TREASURE

For some folks today, the search for treasure is serious, expensive business. The adventure lies in the researching, documenting and pinpointing of a wreck that, just maybe, is laden with a worthwhile cargo. The business begins when any serious thought is given toward excavating or raising the hulk and retrieving its contents.

On a clear day, the salvage efforts of the H.M.S. deBraak can be seen from Cape May Point, across the mouth of the bay in Lewes, Delaware. That operation is indicative of such big business at work.

A few miles north of Cape May, at Ocean City, another ship rests below the sand and surf, and a handful of men have a dream and a plan to venture into the murky depths and recover whatever could be recovered from a giant four-master called the Sindia.

Since beaching in December, 1901, the wreck has fascinated all who have passed by it. A small portion of the ship's tiller still protrudes through the sand, and at low tide some of the Sindia's rotted bulkheads can even be discerned.

Ed Michaud is one who believes the Sindia may hold a small fortune in its clutches. Thousands of pieces of china and assorted goods from the ship's holds were spirited from the wreckage shortly after its grounding, but Michaud believes there could be much, much more a dozen or so feet under the beach.

Bronze, for one thing. Perhaps a massive bronze Buddha, which, at least in popular legend, is said to still be somewhere in the bowels of the big ship.

On this speculation, Michaud and two others have tried to raise the sentiment, the support and the money so they can lower themselves into the Sindia and bring out whatever might be salvageable.

The Sindia was most certainly not a "treasure wreck" by any stretch of the imagination, and any attempt to buck the sand and waves and isolate the ship's innards would be dangerous and expensive. It would be a gamble with worse odds, perhaps, than those afforded by the gleaming casinos just up the next island.

Still, the possibility of digging deep into the Sindia remains an obsession with Michaud. Ed Michaud is a dreamer, but so were others like Burt Webber, Mel Fisher and Robert Ballard. Without those dreams, and the "angels" who helped them come true, the Concepcion, Atocha and Titanic may never have yielded their secrets and their abundance.

Ed Michaud probably wouldn't mind being called a "treasure hunter." An established and respected commercial diver, the Framingham, Massachusetts, native has researched sunken vessels since the age of 13. He has about 25,000 identified or located on charts and in his iron-clad mind. The Sindia is but one of them, but one of the most fascinating. So far, it has given up only a handful of cups and teapots, sucked from a tempest of sand churned up by pumps lowered beneath the sand. Ed Michaud knows—he just knows—that there is more down there.

He knows that there is much more treasure, or at least valuable and salvageable cargo, lining the beaches, creeks and bogs of Cape May. One day, the authors spoke with him near his Ocean City home.

"There are a lot of old wrecks in the bay, close to the shore," he said. "A lot of them are believed to have been victims of pirates. Very interesting wreckage, some of it. Every once in a while, someone finds a gold coin off one of them. Anyway, it's a known fact that Blackbeard was in the area. Kidd, however, was not in the area, ever. At least that's my assumption. He simply didn't have the time.

"I think it was Blackbeard here," Michaud continued. "Blackbeard's first mate was Israel Hand. That's an historical fact. Hand was a misfit, a black sheep, one of six children in Cape May, actually Cold Springs.

"Hand once sailed on a merchant vessel to the Caribbean, and his ship was ransacked by pirates. Well, Israel Hand became a pirate. It was very common in those days. Hand stayed with Blackbeard for his whole career, and it is believed that he convinced Blackbeard to come up to this area.

"It made sense, because all they would have to do is sit in the bay here and watch for the merchantmen's sails as they came down from and up to Philadelphia. Look at the history of the cape. This was uninhabited, all marshland. On the tip of the cape there was a sparce population of whaling men and farmers. Hand used to be a farmer.

"On the Delaware side, there were more settlements, but on the Cape May side it was more barren. They could hide in one of the creeks with their shallow draft vessels and strike quickly. As a result, they'd bring their ships in here, ransack them, and sink them right here. It only made sense, since they figured nobody would trek through the knee-deep marsh and mud unless they knew what they were looking for."

It it interesting to note that in the mid-1940s, an Ocean City man revealed the existence of a tattered and faded document he said would direct the holder to some of Captain Kidd's treasure, buried on a cedar hummock near what is now the Villas.

The man told the press and historical researchers that the small piece of parchment with the directions handwritten on it was passed down through his family for centuries. He said a dying member of Captain Kidd's crew gave it to his great-great-grandfather at the time of the Revolution.

The man's name was Hand. Could it not be that somehow, over the years, the name of the pirate became muddled? Could the "dying member of Captain Kidd's crew" actually have been Israel Hand?

As he looked over the directions to the buried treasure, modern-day treasure hunter Ed Michaud tossed some thoughts out regarding its validity.

"Here, it reads, find the third creek from the cape, go six reaches up the creek on the starboard or southerly side, about 14 perches from the creek, on a small cedar hummock. Probably that cedar hummock could be under a main road. You go up any of these creeks along here and you get up into an area, not of civilization but of marshland. There are some roads that intersect through that marshland, so there's still a chance that that cedar hummock is still there, undisturbed, although it may have been altered in some way by hurricanes, etc. I firmly believe that the treasure is out there. But I, for one, am not willing to risk all the money to look for it."

Michaud thought more about the possible connection of Israel Hand and Blackbeard, and speculated that many of the tales of buried treasure attributed to Captain Kidd might be more logically traced to Blackbeard.

"You look through newspaper articles of that day and there are numerous accounts of ships being ransacked and pulled into this area of the cape. Undoubtably it was Blackbeard, some of his henchmen or some of his crew.

"Israel Hand made many visits to his home," he continued, "and he was kicked out of his house many times. It's in the annals of Cape May. They kicked him out. They knew he was a pirate. The authorities tried to catch him at home one time and missed him.

"As I said, Israel Hand is mentioned in the biographies and stories of Blackbeard, and he is mentioned in the histories of Cape May. It's too coincidental to be just legend. It makes sense that they were one in the same."

Michaud pulled from his files accounts of buried chests of jewels and gold and silver being dug up from Cape May soil in the past century or so, and pointed out that one alleged discovery was made on a farm that was located next to the old Hand homestead.

The 1872 find, it was said, was a money chest attributed to Captain Kidd. "I still don't believe that," was Ed Michaud's confident reaction.

The "treasures" sought by Michaud and those like him are

often not silver, gold or jewels, but seemingly pedantic substances such as copper, coal, or even just plain history!

Michaud's mind spills over with instant knowledge of wrecks that have been forgotten by or never known to others.

"Well, there's the copper pile," he recalled as he began a review of some of the more significant wrecks along the cape. "Very few divers know about it. One boat out of Delaware knows about it. I've been on her once. There's a hell of a pile of copper down there, copper in ingots. They're rectangular and are about a hundred pounds apiece. There's some round pigstyle and some sandcast, Spanish-style from the era of about 1830 to 1850. I'd say there was something like at least a hundred tons of copper there. Evidently she used it as ballast as well as cargo, which made sense. She could carry more that way."

The "copper pile," as Michaud calls it, is in about sixty feet of water directly between the mainland and what he calls the "china wreck."

Almost every stretch of coastline has its "china wreck," and Michaud was quick to point out that there could easily be some confusion about the exact location of the china wreck, because there are three wrecks off the Cape May coast that are commonly dubbed "the china wreck."

"But," he pointed out, "the five fathom wreck does have a lot of china on it. She also has sheets of rolled steel. Most probably carriage parts. Chances are she was coming from Liverpool with a general cargo. The cargo seems to match the Liverpool trade of the time, about 1830 to 1850. She has a load of wagon parts and some brass handles for drawers and latches for furniture, et cetera."

This five-fathom wreck, this particular china wreck, is in about 80 feet of water and has become a popular destination for scuba divers.

"If you dig into the side of the timbers, you'll expose porcelain like you'd never believe. You pull out the bilge plates, you know, and the china will almost spill on you. You've got to take your knife and pry back some of the metal," Michaud pointed out.

There is no positive identification of the ship. "Unless someone finds building specifications to match up with the wreckage," Michaud said, "she will simply remain unknown."

Just north of Cape May Inlet, on Two Mile Beach, is the wreckage of a better-known ship whose remains still may contain a small fortune in porcelain.

"It's the brig Bethany," Michaud said. "She was coming from Hong Kong with more than $600,000 worth of Oriental porcelain. She wrecked on Two Mile Beach on March 9, 1877.

"She was a brig of 800 tons, typical of the round-bow brigs of the late 1700s. She was built much, much later, but built in the old style. She was an American vessel, and Captain Walter Bendell was in command out of New York. The Bethany left New York, delivered oil to Hong Kong, picked up another cargo of novelties, and headed back to the states. It was a voyage much like that of the Sindia.

"The cargo was listed as porcelain, and insured for $600,000. Obviously, it was valued at much more, but they weren't allowed to insure the ships because the porcelain was very fragile."

What's left of the Bethany is still in the surf near Wildwood. "She exists today," Michaud said. "There's some wreckage there. You have to dig down about three or four feet in the sand, but you will get fragments of porcelain. A jet pump should be used. I would like to hit it one of these days. It's close to shore, in about twelve feet of water."

The wreck of the Bethany caused quite a sensation on what was a relatively sparsely-populated stretch of shore in 1877. As the brig hit bottom, her rigging was destroyed and was scattered on the beach. What remained salvageable was purchased by local folks and the rigging and fittings were taken from her. Her hull and cargo simply sank deeper and deeper in the sand.

"Today," said Ed Michaud, "if you were lucky enough to find this wreck uncovered, you might come across cases of un-damaged porcelain. However, as it stands now, it will take a commercial enterprise to excavate it. I'd say that at least fifty percent of her cargo is destroyed as it sits, but the other fifty percent is worth a small fortune, possibly millions."

Over the years, the Bethany has been exaggerated by some into a major "treasure wreck," and some gold coins found near the Cape May Point light house have (erroneously) been attributed to the wreck of the Bethany.

If any gold found on any Cape May beach could be attached correctly to any shipwreck, it would likely be that of the Juno. The Juno is, arguably, the most important of all the ancient wrecks off Cape May, and may someday prove to be the most lucrative.

There were 425 people aboard the Spanish frigate Juno when it sailed from San Juan, Puerto Rico on October 1, 1802.

The 170-foot, 34-gun warship was on her way back along the American coast for a while and then eastward in the trade winds to Spain. Inside her was an estimated twelve tons of silver, and undoubtedly a good amount of gold and silver coinage.

The weather that October was horrible, and the Juno drifted far off course, continuing far north. Stiff winds pelted the ship, swept the mainsail away and pounded away at the very integrity of the vessel.

Flags of distress were hoisted and the bloated frigate struggled for survival.

More than three weeks into the ill-fated voyage, an American ship, the "Favorite," sailed within sight of the Juno. The captains of both ships established communications, and the Favorite assured the Juno that it would stand by in case of the worse, and escort the damaged ship into an American port.

Another savage gale kicked up, and the Favorite was severely damaged. During the storm, she lost sight of the Juno, and when the weather cleared, there was no evidence of the Spanish ship anywhere. Neither the ship nor any of its passengers or cargo was ever seen again.

Ed Michaud disputes that.

"All people perished," he notes. "Not one body washed ashore. Not one body washed ashore at Cape May. Everybody thinks she sank right off Cape May. She did and she didn't. She is not quite in the Delaware Bay on the ocean side of the china wreck. Nobody knows exactly where. If I knew where, I'd be on her right now. It would take a sidescan magnetometer to find her.

Her bell is known to have washed ashore off Lewes, Delaware. At least, a ship's bell did wash ashore about two weeks after the wreck, still attached to the hanging housing hooked onto the deck. Everybody then thought she sank off Lewes. There were even gold coins washing up on the Delaware side for a while. But, you have to understand the currents out there. They are very strong, so you can have a very light coin wash all the way from Cape May to Lewes in a span of ten years. A lot of coins washed up over there, and most folks thought they were from the de-Braak."

In a startling revelation, Michaud theorizes that some of the evidence linked to the deBraak at Lewes may indeed be from the Juno.

"I know it could be from the Juno," Michaud exclaims. "It lies somewhere directly between Lewes and Cape May Point, not quite in the bay, though. It's more at the mouth of the bay. It's just south of the china wreck, I would guess about ten miles south. It's in about 90 to 100 feet of water."

Michaud contends that the Juno may someday be located, and may someday even relinquish her cargo. "It's diveable, and it's there," he says, with the twinkling of a treasure hunter's eye.

That eye sparkles, too, when Ed discusses what has been, to this point, his own private treasure wreck.

"This baby I'll be moving on some day," he confirms. "At this point there's no sense not to relate what I know. If anybody else finds it, fine. More power to 'em!

"Anyway, this is the first time I've ever mentioned this to anyone before. It is the Merrimac. It was named after the Civil War ironclad. It was a clipper ship, built in 1865 by Harrison Loring in Boston. She went 1,200 tons, had very rakish lines and a copper bottom. In 1867, she was sailing from Liverpool, England, to Philadelphia when she hit the bar off Townsends Inlet's south side.

"It was November 20th, and she was carrying a general cargo, that just happened to include 20 tons of silver bullion consigned to Peter Wright and Sons in Philadelphia for commercial use.

"The ship ran aground pretty far out on the bar, about a mile. There were no survivors, and her upper works were totally destroyed. In addition to the silver, she carried 400 tons of zinc ore, 700 tons of brass and an unknown amount of copper. She sank so fast in the sand that nobody could find her. The insurance company spent two years searching for the wreckage."

Michaud says he has positively confirmed the presence of silver in the ship's cargo manifest, and has ascertained that the insurance company gave up trying to locate the hulk and eventually paid the claim.

"It's an interesting story." he says, "The ship was one of the country's finest clipper ships. The Merrimac and the Westmoreland, another of the big and fast clippers, were racing each other across the ocean. The Merrimac went to tack north and she hit the bar during a foggy night. It wasn't rough, there wasn't a bad storm, but it was foggy. There was a bad storm the next day, and that's why she broke up almost immediately."

Michaud says there was an attempt to salvage the hull after the grounding, but it sank so swiftly into the sand that any hopes of salvage were abandoned after a two-year search by insurance company salvors.

The wreckage of the Merrimac would be a major find for any treasure hunter, and Ed Michaud believes he has a good idea about its location and identification. "I've researched every wreck off Townsend's Inlet, thirty-eight of them, and I've got all the building specifications. Not one of them has a copper bottom. The Merrimac had a copper bottom, so if you find a vessel out there with a copper bottom, your odds are about 80 percent that you have found the Merrimac, and maybe 20 tons of silver.

"Someone is going to be diving on one of those wrecks one day and find a piece of silver. They'll say, 'what the hell is this, lead or something?' It will be hard to identify at first."

Ed Michaud hopes he will be the one who will discover the mysterious wreck, and the thought of that possibility lingers with him. "You know, they say there's a wreck out there called the Commonwealth. Steel hull. Well, I'm beginning to wonder if that couldn't be the Merrimac. They say it's a steel hull, but there's not too much of it exposed. We found chinaware on it. And, there's another wreck out there, too that could be the Merrimac. It's hard to say, you know."

THE CONCRETE SHIP
AND "CAPE MAY DIAMONDS"

A rare relic from a true nautical folly rests in underwater repose just off Sunset Beach near Cape May Point.

It is the S.S. Atlantus, and it has been one of Cape May's most interesting and, at times, controversial attractions.

What remains visible of the ship pokes out of the bay water and creates an alluring, somewhat confusing, almost eerie sight.

The ship was the product of good old Yankee ingenuity that, it could be said, backfired. The Atlantus is made of concrete.

During the first world war, steel was in short supply and the federal government decided to experiment with concrete-hulled vessels.

The 3,000-ton, 250-foot ship was the second concrete freighter built. Original plans called for a fleet of more than three dozen like her, but shortcomings in design and durability resulted in only twelve concrete ships ever being launched.

The Liberty Shipbuilding Corporation of Brunswick, Georgia, built the Atlantus and following her commissioning on June 1, 1919, she went into service for about a year.

Following the war, the Atlantus and the rest of the concrete ships were de-commissioned. The Atlantus was stripped of anything valuable and scrapped near Norfolk, Virginia.

A few years later, a Maryland investor bought the useless hulk, and planned to sink it as part of a slip for a ferry boat service he hoped to establish between Cape May and Lewes, Delaware.

The ship was towed to Cape May Point and moored off

shore. On June 8, 1926, a heavy storm ripped the ship from its moorings and cast it adrift. It grounded in about ten feet of water and settled flat into the sandy bottom.

Over the years, one end of the Atlantus has driven deeper into the sand, and her steel has twisted and rusted while her concrete shell has shattered. Her smokestack, visible through the 1930s, finally fell into the water in the early forties.

While swimming or diving around the wreck is today extremely dangerous and prohibited, there was a time when daring young people could easily reach the remains, wander around, and dive from her railings. One young man did so one time, and never emerged from the water. His body was found several days later, far downstream from the wreck.

If the Atlantus was the creation of Yankee ingenuity, then she was also once the victim of it. Years ago, a Philadelphia insurance firm placed an advertisement on the old wreck. This billboard for boat insurance turned into an ad for "Henri's Restaurant" later, much to the chagrin of local historical society members.

Such crass commercializing on board the Atlantus is long gone. Today, the old concrete ship's memory is preserved with some dignity in historical brochures and photographs available at a gift shop on Sunset Beach.

That particular beach, incidentally, is known also for the presence of "Cape May Diamonds." At any given time, visitors can be seen rummaging through the pebbly beach, hoping to scoop up one of the lustrous stones that can be polished to a clear, crystal gleam that makes for lovely and unique jewelry. The stones in the raw can be dull in appearance, and hardly of the precious or even semi-precious category. In fact, they are quartz stones, smoothed by tide and time. Some believe the continual supply of the "gems" has been enhanced by the presence of the conglomerate form of concrete used in the construction of the Atlantus. As bits of the ship break up and crumble in the water, bits of the stones used to mix the concrete become seeds of Cape May Diamonds.

Polished and cut "diamonds" are available at the gift shop at Sunset Beach, as are tumblers for self-polishing.

THE BONES OF THE "MARTIN"

Most people come to Cape May for the sun, sand, shopping and supping. There are bona fide historical attractions on the cape, and some are very visible and visited. The lighthouse at the point, the Physick House and others come quickly to mind.

How many tourists, day trippers or even residents know of the little monument to one of Cape May's shipwrecks? How many have gone to the corner of Lighthouse and Coral Avenues in Cape May Point and have looked at the remains of the British man-of-war "Martin?"

Granted, there's not much left of the old sloop. What's more, some believe the slowly decaying wooden ribs aren't even of the British warship. They say the size and construction doesn't match that of British sloops of the Martin's vintage.

It is still generally accepted that the wreckage is that of the Martin. No one has yet to prove it or disprove it.

The bones of ancient ships rarely have revealed themselves on the beaches of Cape May. For certain, there are dozens of wrecks just under the sand, but few ever show themselves.

On March 5, 1938, the charred ribs of an old wooden ship and a nearby cannonball found on the beach at Cape May Point caused quite a stir.

At first, the ship's remains were identified as those of an old cape whaler. But then, the cannonball was discovered near the wreck and new theories surfaced. The rusty, 12-pound ball was thought to be from the Revolutionary War era, and the ship might have been a privateer or whaler-turned-warship.

Others speculated that the variety of wood used in the construction of the vessel was indicative of that of a common merchantman, or perhaps even a pirate ship from the Caribbean.

The sea at the point has long since reclaimed the old hulk, and the questions raised during her brief appearance have also faded into the murky depths of time.

The Martin, or what is left of her, met a more noble destiny. When Hurricane Hazel ripped the sands apart in 1954, the ghostly timbers of the ship's underbelly were bared for a new generation to see.

It is believed that the exposure marked the first time in 142 years that any part of the sloop saw the light of day. The H.M.S. Martin was one of about one hundred British sloops or frigates stationed off America's east coast during the War of 1812. A plaque erected at the site tells the story:

> THIS WRECK IS BELIEVED TO BE THE REMAINS OF THE BRITISH SLOOP OF WAR "MARTIN." SHE BLOCKADED THE DELAWARE BAY IN THE WAR OF 1812. SHE WAS ATTACKED IN 1812, DRIVEN ON THE SHOALS AND BURNT, DRIFTING TO CAPE MAY POINT. SHE BECAME BURIED IN THE SAND FOR OVER A CENTURY. EXPOSED IN 1954, THE MARTIN WAS SALVAGED AND MOUNTED HERE IN THE PUBLIC INTEREST. GEORGE PETTINGS AND THE CAPE MAY DEVELOPMENT COMPANY.

Since placed on public display, some of the weatherbeaten remains of the Martin's frame have fallen prey to souvenir hunters and vandals. There are still wooden pegs visible, and it is easy to imagine the massive, majestic vessel that once rose above the forlorn skeleton.

Elsewhere, the cadaverous framework might be better protected. Similar remains of ancient ships can be seen in the enclosed confines of maritime museums. The elements, and society itself can prove to be destructive to the valuable wreckage in coming years, and perhaps the craggy old pieces of wood should be placed in more secure surroundings and in a more dramatic setting. In too few years, for too many reasons, the treasured link with the past may be broken.

Men once lived, worked, sang, danced, fought and died on the decks that were once above those craggy old pieces of wood. You can stand next to them today, close your eyes, shut off the sounds around you and ponder. You can almost hear the distant roar of cannons, the shuffle of a hundred feet. You can almost hear those craggy old pieces of wood creaking again as the sea pushes and pulls against them. You can almost sense that those craggy old pieces of wood are somehow back out there on the bay, and you're there, too.

That's the kind of feeling that should never be allowed to pass, and the Martin's craggy old pieces of wood are the kinds of artifacts that should never be allowed to simply rot away into oblivion.

ONLY HER NAME REMAINS

As shipwrecks go, the wreck of the Johan Lang is unremarkable. The sturdy schooner was sailing back to Philadelphia, and had just sighted the Five Fathoms Lightship at Cape May. The coastline was on the horizon, and the long voyage that included stops in Bordeaux, France and ports in Finland was near its end.

Aboard the ship were the captain, his wife and son, and a crew of 14. Their names have faded into obscurity. In fact, precious little is known about the Johan Lang itself, other than on November 24, 1877, it succumbed to heavy seas off shore. The vessel took water and began to list precariously.

A Life-saving crew was quick to respond to the foundering ship, and despite the rolling waves encountered along the way, they managed to rescue all hands.

What has etched the name of the Johan Lang forever in Cape May history is the fact that after the ship was abandoned, it washed steadily toward the beach, eventually coming on shore on the north shoal of the Hereford Inlet. Somehow, one of its name boards was salvaged, and it is now on display in the maritime history collection of the Cape May County Historical Museum near Cape May Court House.

Near the Lang's nameboard, incidentally, is another interesting piece of local maritime lore. It is one of the relics usually pointed out by tour guides and it could be called a trophy of sorts to a most unusual "rum runner."

It is a model of the brig, "J.B. Kirby," which was on a voyage to Cienfugus, Cuba with Captain Hiram Godfrey as its master in 1860. During the trip, Captain Godfrey, who resided on Cape May, contracted Yellow Fever and died.

The Kirby's first mate, a Mr. Beading, took command and brought the ship back from the Caribbean with a most unusual "cargo" in its hold.

In order to escape the rigors of quarantine when reaching its American port, the Kirby's interim master decided to hide the deceased captain's corpse. He placed Godfrey's body inside a cask of rum and evaded the authorities!

The model that is on display today at the historical museum was made by Hiram W. Godfrey, son of the sea captain who came home in a cask.

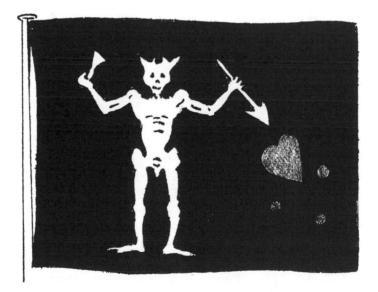

A BAD DAY ON THE BEACH

In the days when sail was giving way to steam, and when all sorts of ships were following coastal courses with their variety of cargoes, it was not unusual to hear about a wreck somewhere near or on Cape May every few weeks.

Indeed, maritime disasters large and small, involving loss of life, ship or cargo, were so commonplace that the newspapers of the day list them in a manner that today's papers give accounts of automobile accidents.

Such was the case in The New York Times, which in its "Quadruple Sheet," five-cent edition on Sunday, September 24, 1882, reported two Cape May shipwrecks under the heading of "Disasters To Vessels."

One was the Nuphar, a steamer headed to Philadelphia from North Shields, England, loaded with pig iron and drugs. The iron-hulled vessel was built in England the year before at a cost of $200,000, and her cargo was estimated to be worth $50,000.

The Nuphar grounded on the outer bar of Townsend Inlet during a freak storm that saw temperatures drop 18 degrees and more than an inch and a half of rain fall within minutes. Winds kicked up to gusts of over forty miles per hour, and the crew of the Nuphar was caught unaware.

The ship settled into the sand, blocking the entrance to the inlet and thus taking the brunt of the pounding surf. The tug, Argus, arrived on the scene of the wreck to lighten the Nuphar of a portion of her cargo, and Life-Saving crews rescued all hands. The ship, battered and broken by the storm, was left to the salvors.

The same story included the account of the beaching of the Austrian bark Antonion Mimbelli, which was another victim of the autumn storm.

The big sailing ship was cast ashore on the southern end of Two Mile Beach, and once out of her seaborne element, went immediately to pieces. The waves smashed her relatively delicate wooden hull as she, too lay beam to the wind just off the beach.

The Mimbelli was in ballast from New York to the Delaware Breakwater, and her crew was saved by Life-Savers. The ship was a total loss, but her valuable rigging was dismantled and salvaged.

BLINDED BY THE LIGHT

Normally, a buoy, lighthouse or lightship is a beacon of safety and guidance for those at sea. But for the 170-foot, 1,900-ton schooner, "City of Georgetown," the old Five Fathoms Bank Lightship, which once marked the entrance to the Delaware Bay off Cape May, was a glare of gloom.

The wind was fickle and the night was cold and dark on February 3, 1913. The City of Georgetown, an 11-year-old four-master built in the storied yards of Bath, Maine, was coasting south with her holds full of sugar bound from New York to Savannah, Georgia.

Her captain, A.J. Slocum, had taken a course close to the shore. The City of Georgetown marked her position from coastal light to light, buoy to buoy, landmark to landmark. It seemed a safe enough way of groping down the coast and staying out of the way of the big steamers that were plying the shipping lanes farther out.

The helmsman and lookouts marked another leg of their voyage by spotting the bright light of the Five Fathoms Lighship in the distance. They knew by this sighting that they were just off Cape May and would soon be sailing by the wide mouth of the Delaware Bay.

At about the same time, the big Hamburg-American liner "Prinz Oskar" was cruising past the Delaware Breakwater. Its deck men, too, had noticed the familiar glow of the lightship in the distance, and they knew that it meant the ship would soon leave the bay and enter the trans-Atlantic lane.

The time was just after midnight, and no one on either ship had any inkling of what was to happen. For both crews on watch, it was a quiet, albeit frigid, night, and the distant lightship represented a certain kind of security.

The City of Georgetown felt her way closer to the lightship, her helmsman very aware that it was stationed at a somewhat busy crossroads of maritime traffic. All precautions against any unforeseen events were taken.

The Prinz Oskar began her wide sweep around the lightship, and set a course for the open sea.

The light from the Five Fathoms Bank Lightship carried across the waves more than twenty miles. It was one of the brightest of all along the coast. That distinction, on that cold February night, was to contribute to the demise of the City of Georgetown.

At about five minutes before one in the morning, the big liner made her turn around the lightship and most eyes were on that vessel.

Suddenly a lookout on the bow of the Prinz Oskar screamed in horror that a sailing ship was dead ahead. "Reverse engines . . . full speed astern," was the immediate order from the bridge as the ship's signal bells clanged frantically.

On the City of Georgetown, a terrified helmsman looked up, and through the glaring, overpowering whiteness of the lightship's beam, he made out the silhouette of the big liner's bow. Fully aware that it was far too late, still he shouted for the sails to be cut loose. At the same instant, he whipped his wheel around in a futile effort to avoid the inevitable.

The deck hands aboard the schooner responded as quickly as humanly possible, but it was to no avail. As the ship wheeled around, a gust of wind pumped into the sails. The schooner accelerated, and her prow thrust forward, into the giant, steel steamer.

The force was incredible. The bowsprit plunged through the steel plates like a pencil through paper. The steamer's anchor was shoved several feet back into the forecastle, and throughout the ship, crewmen and passengers were shaken violently from their sleep.

Aboard the ill-fated schooner, chaos reigned supreme. At the moment of impact, the four tall masts tottered and crumbled onto the deck. There was rigging, sails and spars everywhere. Captain Slocum and his seven men were caught in a tangle of wood, canvas and rope that threatened their very lives.

Although shaken by the crash, all 33 passengers and the crew of the Oskar were safe. Some passengers, upon hearing the crunch and the wildly-ringing signal bells, had emerged from their cabins in a panic, but were quickly assured that all was well aboard the liner.

All was definitely not well aboard the City of Georgetown. The schooner's wood and the liner's steel were momentarily melded together after the collision, and the schooner seemed to maintain some semblance of seaworthiness.

But as the reversed engines of the liner pulled the bigger ship free from the clutch of collision, it was immediately obvious that the sailing ship was in deep peril.

The blinding light of the lightship illuminated the scene with an eerie, shadowy brilliance. This normally welcoming light could now only serve to illuminate a tragedy.

The desperate crew of the City of Georgetown rocked with their vessel as the liner jerked herself free. Trying to fight through the wreckage on the schooner's deck, they looked in amazement as the liner pulled away. In an instant, the sailing ship began to go down at the bow. Icy water surged onto the main deck, and the ship began to swirl around in its death throes.

Four men managed to launch the dory and began to row while the other four grasped the dory's gunwales. The scene was still very confusing and horrifying, as the schooner whirled ever downward. This maelstrom sucked in all around it. Wreckage was spinning everywhere, and soon the pull of the whirlpool claimed even the men who were clinging precariously to the little dory.

The four men grasped for anything that would keep them afloat. Helplessly, the other four on the dory watched. Squinting through the blaze of the lightship, they could see that the Prinz Oskar had launched its lifeboats. It would be a matter of which would claim the four men—the whirlpool or the lifeboats.

Crewmen from the liner pulled hard and fast to reach the victims. The strength of both those on the lifeboats and those clinging to the flotsam for dear life was rapidly draining in the cold night. Somehow, though, the lifeboats reached the victims in time, and all were plucked from the sea and brought safely aboard.

From the lifeboat and from the dory, the men of the City of Georgetown watched as their ship slipped beneath the waves.

The men were saved, and the Prinz Oskar, after repairs, was returned to service.

But some forty miles off the Cape, the Five Fathoms Bank Lightship, until it was replaced by the present light buoy, stood vigil over the wreckage of the City of Georgetown. In a freak accident, the schooner was destroyed by the same light that was meant to guide and protect her.

THE HOODOO SHIP

Some vessels seem to be jinxed. The steamer "Northern Pacific" could be considered one of them.

Built in 1914 in the Cramp Shipyards of Philadelphia, the 8,500-ton steamer made a rather clumsy entrance. As she headed south in the Delaware River preparing for sea trials off the coast of Maine, she went aground just south of League Island in the Philadelphia harbor.

Still, the ship eventually passed the tests and was actually hailed as the fastest and finest turbine-driven steamship built in the United States up to that time.

She and her sister ship, the Great Northern, were designed to run cargo and passengers from Astoria, Oregon, to San Francisco. For a period, she did just that. Then, her owners put her on the San Francisco-Honolulu route, where she served admirably.

When America's involvement in World War I was increased, the swift Northern Pacific was enlisted into the Cruiser/ Transport Squadron and refitted in Bremerton, Washington.

Under the command of Lieutenant Commander Alfred Hunter, the ship sailed from the West Coast through the Panama Canal to New York harbor and reported for duty as a support ship.

The steamer racked up a proud record during the war, serving chiefly as a troop transport between Hoboken, New Jersey, and Brest, France. But her problems, and her reputation as what sailors would call a "hoodoo ship" had just begun.

On one of her 13 trans-Atlantic voyages, the influenza epidemic that had decimated humanity made its presence felt aboard the Northern Pacific.

It was September, 1918, with hundreds of returning soldiers and casualties from Europe, when the flu infested the ship. Seven men died.

It was not the first time that sickness had crippled the ship's operations. Three years earlier, while still a civilian steamer, a smallpox epidemic broke out on the Northern Pacific and necessitated a long quarantine for her 400 passengers in San Diego, California.

The misfortune seemed to spread to her sister ship. In October, 1918, the Great Pacific, in convoy with the Northern, was damaged in a collision with a British ship and had to be escorted by her sister vessel.

While still serving the Navy on January 1, 1919, the Northern Pacific was completing a voyage from France when she ran aground in fog on Fire Island, Long Island, New York. Aboard were some 2,400 soldiers and officers returning from the war zones. About 1,700 of them were injured men, and rescue parties from the Coast Guard had a difficult time getting the injured personnel off the ship.

These relatively minor incidents could easily be overlooked, however, because of the Northern Pacific's outstanding record of wartime service.

By August, 1919, her Navy responsibilities were completed, and she was turned over to the Army Transport Service. There would be more honorable duty, and more bad luck.

On January 20, 1920, while bringing the very last contingent of American forces back from France, the radio room of the Northern Pacific picked up an S.O.S. from the steamer Powhatan, which was in distress off the coast of Nova Scotia. The Northern Pacific altered its course and took the disabled vessel's passengers to New York.

Later that year, the Northern Pacific was selected to take General John J. Pershing on a trip through the Antilles and the Caribbean. As fate would have it, however, she ran aground once again. This time, it was at a very strategic part of the entrance to the harbor of San Juan, Puerto Rico. The beached ship closed and clogged the harbor for several days until she was freed from the sandbar.

The Northern Pacific was finished with its service to the nation by late 1921, and was purchased from the government by the Admiral Line for a million dollars. She would be sent back to more docile duty, once again as a West Coast steamer.

Meanwhile, her sister ship, Great Pacific, continued to serve the military as the Naval Administrative Flagship Columbia.

The Northern Pacific was relegated to a lonely pier in Hoboken for several months after her decomissioning. What was the nation's fastest troopship was a forgotten and forlorn hulk until the Admiral Line realized her worth.

As they prepared the ship for her new assignment, and her new name—the "H.F. Alexander,"—the new owners decided to have her reconditioned in the Sun Shipbuilding Co. yards in Chester, Pennsylvania.

The ship was in tow and bound for Chester when her illustrious life came to a fiery, fatal end. The Northern Pacific was twenty miles off Cape May on February 8, 1922, when all hell broke loose.

The night was frightful. Winds of fifty knots churned the sea to a frenzied mass of towering waves and snow blinded the men on watch on the bridge.

Second Officer A.B. Wilson was on deck for the midnight watch, and was doing his best to guide the ship through the rough storm. The mouth of the Delaware Bay and some shelter was close by, and the Northeast End Lightship would have been visible under clearer conditions.

Wilson's concerns about the storm were dwarfed by what was to come.

"I was on watch on the bridge," he told investigators after the incident. "The stiff wind which was hitting us broadside brought me a whiff of smoke. I ran to the saloon deck, opened a door and found the cabins and saloons full of smoke. As I entered the companionway leading to the lower deck, the flames burst forth in a seething mass."

Wilson woke the captain and immediately ordered the lifeboats lowered and an S.O.S. to be sent from the radio room.

"NORTHERN PACIFIC AFIRE AND HELPLESS . . .

PLEASE SEND HELP!"

The message was received as a faint but obviously frantic call by an unsuspecting wireless operator at the Cape May Naval Air Station. Within moments, the crew of the Coast Guard cutter Kickapoo was mustered. Another report of a ship on fire came in from a northbound tanker, and yet another dispatch came in from the merchantman Herbert G. Wylie, which reported that the fire was consuming the unknown vessel quickly.

Civilian and military doctors were called quickly to accompany the Coast Guards to the scene.

Ships in the area of the burning Northern Pacific rallied to the aid of the stricken vessel's crew. The Wylie was joined by the steamer "Lake Fabian" and freighter "Transportation" for any possible rescue operations.

Captain Seth Chase of the Transportation, detailed the scene upon his ship's arrival. "The sea was very rough," he noted, "but we had no trouble picking up three boats. When we first sighted the Northern Pacific she was in flames from end to end. We made all speed to her assistance and found the lifeboats floating about the burning vessel.

"The rescue work was completed in about an hour. The Northern Pacific, listing about 30 degrees, was still afloat."

The big two-stacker was fully involved in flames. "Because of the quick spread of the flames," Second Officer Wilson said, "we had great difficulty in launching the boats. We tried at first to get them over the leeward side, but found this impossible. We then tried to get them over the windward side, a much more dangerous proceeding. We got the boats launched, however, thanks to the splendid seamanship and bravery of both officers and men, and every one of the crew got away safely. Several of the men were singed by the flames as we launched the boats."

The Northern Pacific was manned by a skeleton crew of 27 men, a far cry from the wartime complement of nearly 300. Also aboard for the short trip to the shipyard were two draftsmen, an engineer and a carpenter from the Sun Shipbuilding Company. They were on the ship to take preliminary measurements and make plans for the half-million dollar rebuilding job at Chester.

These four men became the last victims of the "hoodoo ship."

Wilson's testimony included his thoughts on how the four men lost their lives. "When the lifeboat I commanded was launched," he said, "there was no sign of the four shipyard employees. They had not come on deck, and sailors had been unable to reach their quarters. I believe the fire started near the place where these four men were sleeping."

The raging blaze on the ship was believed to have been started by an oil tank leak. The ship was still carrying some 7,500 barrels of oil from her last wartime assignment. The shipyard workers were apparently sleeping near the origin of the fire and were trapped.

The inferno on the Northern Pacific continued for hours, and those who observed the tragedy marvelled at the ship's resilience. Wilson said, "The ship was burning from bow to superstructure. That was at seven o'clock in the morning. The intense heat was cracking the ship's plates, causing them to open up and let in the sea. The vessel listed heavily. It is remarkable that she remained on top of the waves until yesterday afternoon."

That "yesterday afternoon" reference was made to the hour of three o'clock, when the Northern Pacific rolled over slowly and slipped down through 21 fathoms of sea water to her final resting place. The burning paint sizzled and the floating firebrand shot billows of steam into the chilly air as the sinking of the ship extinguished the blaze.

Captain W.J. Hutson of the Coast Guard's Kickapoo said he'd never seen a hotter or more ominous fire on an vessel, ever. He said the Northern Pacific was so intensely hot and the flames aboard her so volatile that his cutter was forced to stay a quarter of a mile away at all times.

The Kickapoo and other rescue ships stayed with the Northern Pacific for the hours it remained afloat, like a fiery Viking funeral boat. Captain Hutson said the former troop transport drifted about 35 miles until it eventually sank. All the while, a keen eye was kept on and around the ship for any signs of the four shipyard workers who were missing.

The survivors of the conflagration were taken to Newport News, Virginia, by the ships that saved them. The radio operator of the Wylie had one more grim task to perform, however. After the hours of fruitless searching, he tapped out the final passage in the saga of the Northern Pacific. To the Sun Shipbuilding Company, the following: "HAVE NOT YOUR MEN ABOARD. WHEN LEFT SCENE OF DISASTER THERE WAS NO TRACE OF LIFE ANYWHERE."

FIRE IN THE BAY

It was not a very good year at all for the Delaware Bay, and especially for the Clyde Line.

On January 2, 1925, the sleek liner "Mohawk," the pride of the Clyde Line of passenger/cargo ships, was en route from New York to Jacksonville, Florida, with 207 passengers and 80 crew members. The passengers were almost all headed back to the resort hotels of the Sunshine State after the holidays, ready but perhaps not willing to resume their wintertime jobs. The northerners departed New York Harbor on New Year's Day and were only hours out of port when the first reports of impending disaster were received.

The captain was told that a fire was burning below, and was spreading quickly.

Outside, sleet and driving snow whipped by swirling winds created an icy, bitter maelstrom. Inside, the Mohawk was a sweltering inferno. There were some very critical decisions to be made.

At first, the crew felt it could contain the fire. That was at about 7 p.m. By midnight, it appeared that the blaze had spread too far, and extraordinary measures had to be taken.

Wisely, the captain decided to steer the million-dollar, 17-year old, Philadelphia-built liner into the comparatively sheltered confines of the Delaware Bay and hopefully into the little harbor at Lewes, Delaware.

For various reasons, refuge at Lewes was not possible. The next best thing, the captain reasoned, was to seek safety near a recognizable spot in the bay.

The Mohawk cleared Cape May at about 3 a.m., and already local Coast Guards were being scrambled to come to the liner's assistance.

"At 3 o'clock we cleared the end of the jetties at the mouth of Cold Spring Inlet. In all of my thirty-five years experience at sea I have never been aboard a vessel that bobbed around so in the seas, which then were terribly high, every wave dashing clear over the pilot house and reminding one of a boiling cauldron."

The words were those of Captain Hayes of the cutter Kickapoo, who lauded the Mohawk's captain's seamanship. "I want to give all the praise in the world to Captain Staples of the Mohawk," he said. "If, when he found that his ship was on fire, he had attempted to breach the fifty-mile gale, and tried to return to New York, in less than one hour the Mohawk would have been burned to the water's edge and in the raging seas off the coast no boat from the Mohawk would have lived over three minutes."

The rescue ships found the Mohawk just off the Brandywine Shoals, the liner's hull hopelessly beyond control. The fire was steaming in her holds, the bay water was beginning to rush in her splitting seams, and she was at a perilous 45-degree list.

Surprisingly, the initial panic among her passengers had subsided, and all were safely removed from the Mohawk after nearly fifteen hours of literal hell.

The rescue was not without its incidents. Two cats and a dog, the ship's mascots, perished, but all humans were saved. The passengers and crew were lowered to the smaller rescue vessels with the help of Jacob's ladders, but for one man such an arrangement would never do.

Unable to negotiate the tricky ladders, one man who weighed an estimated 400 pounds, was rolled from liner to cutter on a wide, sturdy plank.

Almost left behind in the rescue operations were two members of a Vaudeville team. They had been sleeping throughout the entire emergency, but rolled out of their beds when the ship began to list. They awoke to an abandoned ship, ran through the passageways to the decks, waved their arms wildly and screamed, and were rescued.

Captain Staples wrestled with his decisions, and as the passengers and crew made their way off the doomed liner, he pondered the cause of the fire. There were 50 automobiles and 1,800 tons of general cargo on board, but nothing volatile enough to spark such a major blaze.

But in the waning moments in the life of the Mohawk, the captain had little time to think. It was clear that the sea, or in this case the bay, would claim another victim. The seacocks of the 368-foot "pride of the line" were opened, the captain bowed his head, looked up and climbed a ladder to safety.

The Mohawk simmered and settled into 40 feet of water between the Brandywine Shoals and Fourteen Foot Bank Lights. At dawn, on Cape May's western shore, townspeople gathered to watch the end of the Mohawk and wait for any random flotsam and jetsam that might wash up on the beach.

The passengers who were headed for Florida were taken to Wilmington to resume their journey, by train.

Another Clyde liner would have another fiery date with the Delaware Bay late in 1925. The "Lenape" was on the same New York-Jacksonville route as the Mohawk, and met her fate in much the same fashion as the Mohawk.

Late in the evening of November 17, fire was discovered in the aft hold of the Lenape as she steamed just off Five Fathoms Light.

"I cannot understand how the fire started," a perplexed and crestfallen Captain Charles Devereaux said following the disaster. "I am thankful that we were so fortunate to escape without heavy loss of life. Perhaps the fire might not have gained such headway had we slowed down after it was discovered. But I considered it my duty to consider by passengers first, even at the cost of my ship."

There were 367 souls on board the Lenape, and all but one were rescued. The only casualty was a man who panicked and leaped from the deck into smoky waters even as the lifeboats were being lowered. His body was found later on the morning of November 18.

The Lenape was scuttled just off Lewes, Delaware, in twenty feet of water, and allowed to burn herself out. The total loss, ship, 1,500 tons of cargo (and 49 automobiles) was estimated at $2 million.

An interesting sidebar to the story of the Lenape is that 17 members of her crew had survived yet another Clyde Lines ship fire, that of the "Comanche," off Mayport, Florida, the previous month.

What's more, Joseph Knibbs, the Lenape's butcher (described by the contemporary press as "a phlegmatic and stolid negro"), had not only gone through the fires of the Lenape and the Comanche, but he had also been on the crew of the Mohawk when it burned in the Delaware Bay earlier in the year.

Reporters asked Knibbs if the three disasters in one year, working for one company, would deter him from going back to sea.

"Sure I'm going back," he replied. "It's my occupation. When your time comes you die anyway, so it's no use being scared."

Knibbs, who played a key role in fighting the fire aboard the Lenape, added, "When you come off with your life in this business, you ought to be happy. I ought to be getting used to this kind of thing."

THE WRECK OF THE BILLY DIGGS

This is really a wreck on a wreck. Officially the "William B. Diggs," the wreck some 8 miles off the east jetty light of Cape May Harbor is known to local fishermen and divers as the "Billy Diggs."

The Diggs was an oak, 1,041-ton barge built in April, 1918 by a Maryland shipbuilder, and went down in 1934 during an attempt to salvage a wreck.

According to information supplied by Joe Harrison, of the commercial diving and underwater salvage firm in Cape May that bears his name, divers were attempting to salvage the unknown wreck from the Diggs when a nor'easter swirled suddenly. The barge apparently sprang a leak and sank.

The barge slithered through fifty feet of water and settled on top of the other wreckage. Following the demise of the Diggs, a buoy with a blinking green light was placed at the site. That gave rise to another popular nickname for the wreck, the "Green Light Blinker." That buoy was removed in the 1970s, and the wreckage was blown apart for navigational purposes.

Today, the wreckage lies about a mile southeast of buoy 3FB, and is very interesting for scuba divers.

Most notable is the preponderance of growth of yellow sulphur sponge that covers and colors the Billy Diggs. In addition, a large anchor, some eight feet across the fluke, is very visible. So, too, are a pair of tapered metal funnels, said to resemble crucibles at a steel mill.

Harrison says there is much to be seen at and around the wreck of the Billy Diggs, and the sea bass and blackfish just love the place!

The common occurrence of finding random wreck sites known by divers as "The China Wreck" (because china dishes were retrieved from it) or "The Billy Diggs" (a corruption of the vessel's actual name) is an interesting phenomenon.

Around Cape May, serious divers have attached some rather frivolous, capricious and sometimes baffling sobriquets to the wrecks down below.

The "Crybaby Wreck" is so named, legend has it, because it was once the private domain of one fisherman who discovered it, and fished about it with great success. When he arrived at the location of his own, private wreck-reef one day and saw another boat haulin' 'em in, he cried.

The "Junkie" wreck was given its name because of the useless and unidentifiable junk that has been pulled from it.

One wreck off the coast is known as the "Meat Wreck." Local divers say it got the name because of the huge volume of sea bass caught around it.

The "Bell Wreck" earned its monicker after a brass ship's bell was plucked from it, and the "Teaser" wreck is called that because of the lobsters that hide deep within its nooks and crannies, "teasing" would-be lobster-pluckers.

And then, there are wreck nicknames that defy any logical explanation, although readers are welcome to provide their own.

Some great sailing ship, perchance, now lies at the door to Davy Jones' Locker, anonymously on the bottom of the sea, and is known by local divers as the "Slop Wreck."

Another once-proud clipper, perhaps a fleet three-master that set speed records on the high seas from Madagascar to Malay, eventually found her last resting place on the undersea sands off Cape May.

In life, her creamy sails bulged with pride. In death, the divers caller the "$1.50 Wreck."

Life sometimes just ain't fair, even for ships!

TALES OF "RUM ROW"

One of the most interesting, colorful, embarrassing and tragic periods of American history, and indeed, Cape May history, is the time between the 18th and 21st amendments to the U.S. Constitution.

Prohibition, 1920 to 1933.

Any account of "bootlegging" or "rum running" along the New Jersey coastline during these years when the manufacturing, sale or importation of intoxicating liquors within the borders of the United States was prohibited would be a book unto itself.

Up and down the coast there are myriad tales of how the local citizenry managed to bring booze into speakeasies and homes despite the vigilance of the Coast Guard and other federal law enforcers. Some of those accounts border on the comical, while some are tragic.

Off Cape May, as along most points along America's shores, there was a state of war between the rum-runners and the authorities. The law pretended to rid the nation of the evil liquids, but the people would not be denied.

Home stills and backyard breweries popped up everywhere. Bathtub gin found its ways into clubs where the illicit beverages were consumed behind very closed doors.

There were stills and speakeasies on Cape May, according to one man who was on the government's side in the struggle between those who would have liquor and those who would deny it to them.

Ralph Clayton Sr., had the distinct honor of serving in the U.S. Coast Guard during the height of Prohibition, and he remembers it well.

He remembers sloshing through a bay marsh with a revolver in his teeth, under fire being returned by rum-runners who leaped from a 30-foot motor cruiser loaded with 115 cases of liquor. Despite the pursuit, the four criminals escaped.

Clayton also remembers that being a Coast Guardsman in those days was not the most pleasant task. At times, it was a case of brother-against-brother, friend-against-friend, all in the name of keeping alcohol away from Americans.

On Cape May, the average rum-runner was nothing more than an opportunistic fisherman out for a fast buck. There was a very good chance that the fisherman-turned-bootlegger knew the local Coast Guardsman well, and the confrontations in the name of the law were awkward. Ralph Clayton says the Coast Guardsmen were not well liked at the time, and were often the targets of threats and acts of violence.

ITEM: ATLANTIC CITY PRESS, WEDNESDAY AUGUST 23, 1933

HEADLINE: RUM CHASER BOMBED

CAPE MAY, Aug. 22 (AP)—An unsuccessful attempt was made early today to blow up the Hiawatha, coast guard chaser of the Cape May Station.

The craft, which crashed into and sank a 50-foot alleged rum runner in Delaware Bay last Friday, was damaged slightly.

Coast Guard officials said they believed two sticks of dynamite were hurled at the Hiawatha, which has been on the Marine Railway at Schellenger's Landing for repairs since the crash. The explosive tore a large hole in the ground and damaged a portion of the fence surrounding the railway.

Authorities expressed the belief the dynamite was thrown by rum runners. They said they believe it was hurled either from mud flats surrounding the marine railway, or from a boat.

H.A. Pederson, chief motor machinist, who has been on guard at the landing since the coast guard chaser was brought here, said he had just gone off duty for the day and that "suddenly a flare lighted the flats, and there was a loud explosion."

"The ground shook and I could hear broken glass falling," he said. "The blast came from the port side of the railway. I think the dynamite must have been hurled from the flats."

Ralph Clayton says there were other incidents similar to the bombing of the Hiawatha, especially in the latter months and weeks of Prohibition.

In the beginning, when Americans were only learning how to circumvent the law, the process was haphazard and primitive.

"Down along this part of the Jersey shore," says Clayton, "the vessels lay at what was called 'rum row,' beyond the three mile limit."

"I remember that one time, I believe there were twelve vessels laying off this area. Then, you could get in your boat and you could get the liquor over the rail, by the case. But that didn't last too long, because then the government, the Coast Guard, started to enforce it. Then, they dug up an old law that our territorial limit extended up to twelve miles off. So, rum row moved out to twelve miles. But then it was not possible to buy over the rail anymore."

Clayton says the ease of off-shore booze buying and the romance of rum row disappeared when syndicates took over the lucrative business of rum running.

To combat more sophisticated bootlegging, the Coast Guard itself was forced to take more serious measures. In 1923, what was called the "Dry Navy" formed at nearby Atlantic City. The mother ship "Pickering" along with sixteen patrol boats and nine smaller crafts were dispatched to the legal limits off shore, and braced themselves for some no-moments encounters with the clever lawbreakers who, in Clayton's words, "could do the bay blindfolded!"

The former World War I submarine chasers "Hiawatha" and "Kickapoo" operated out of Cape May, where the Coast Guardsmen were either "L" or "C", surfmen or seamen. The "L" section was the direct descendant of the Life-Savers, while the "C" men were those who served on the swift patrol cutters. Clayton was a "C" man.

At many spots on the shore, there were reports of Coast Guardsmen being "dirty." They were accused of, and convicted of, actually participating in rum running. Clayton cannot remember any of the Cape May Coast Guardsmen falling prey to such temptations. He readily acknowledges, however, that some of the men who fought valiantly against the rum runners by day would wander into area speakeasies after hours. The name of the New World Cafe in Atlantic City still brings a twinkle to Clayton's eye.

Another Cape May man does recall some courts martial after an incident when Coast Guard personnel broke into confiscated booze and had their own party.

He is Frank Rutherford, Jr., long-time mayor of Cape May Point, who was a youngster when Prohibition went into effect. Still, the memories are vivid.

"At night, when we were small kids," he recalls, "my father used to walk us down to the beach. We'd hear the pounding-thumping sound. It was the Coast Guard boats shooting at rum runners. So, we'd go to the beach and watch what happened. We could watch boats burn on the beach after the action."

The action was likely to be hot and heavy at times, since after the Dry Navy's machine-gun-equipped patrol boats were deployed along the cape, the bootleggers armed their ships in kind.

"One time," Rutherford says, "a boat was beached a mile or so above Sunset Beach. The word got out that the boat was there, with its cargo intact. So, a bunch of local people walked up and each one picked up a case. They walked back to Sunset Beach with their booze and sure enough, there was a Coast Guard truck there. The people had to put the stuff into the truck."

The incident the mayor remembers might very well have been the April 4, 1932, grounding of the rum boat "Tuna" between North Highlands Beach and Miami Beach, on the bay side of the cape.

The boat, out of Philadelphia, apparently picked up her load of liquor from one of the three larger ships that were stationed just outside the twelve-mile limit at the time. Each of these "mother" ships had aboard her an estimated 12,000 cases of liquor. Most of it came from infamous bootleg ports such as Lunenberg, Nova Scotia, and Bimini, a Caribbean island.

There were about 300 cases of booze—Canadian Golden Wedding, Lincoln Inn, and several French cordial varieties—on the Tuna when it ran aground. Some of it had already been pilfered by local folks.

The estimated three to five crewmen of the rum runner were long gone when Cape May County Sheriff William B. Powell and his posse of county and state lawmen were tipped off to the beaching of the rum boat. They found a seriously damaged small boat, looking somewhat like a government rum chaser, according to those on the scene.

What they did not find were several cases of liquor, taken away earlier by thirsty Cape May residents.

THE FROZEN GRIP OF DEATH

Duty on board one of the hundreds of schooner barges that were towed up and down the coast in the early part of the twentieth century was not the epitome of the "romance of the sea." It was inglorious, thankless and gruelling work by any standards, and extremely dangerous by some.

The crusty barges, usually the hulls of sailing ships stripped of their masts and rigging, carried mundane cargoes and were at the mercy of a relatively thin lifeline that kept them attached to their tow ship.

The annals of shipwrecks along the New Jersey coast are thick with accounts of these floating workhorses' umbilical cords being severed or snapped. Once cast awash in the open sea, the barges lacked any substantial seaworthiness, and were easily capsized.

Those who seek adventurous, dramatic tales of shipwrecks and sea tragedies may overlook or ignore barge wrecks. Still, they have accounted for innumerable deaths and intolerable agony over the years.

A vivid example of this agony and death was the loss of the schooner barge Carroll, which went to its watery grave off Cape May in mid-February, 1930.

A nondescript 1,280-ton barge that was owned by the Eastern Transportation Company of Baltimore, the Carroll was in tow along with the Hooper and Hallowell behind Montrose, from the Edward Card towboat fleet of New York.

The mid-winter sea was furious, and the Montrose's burden drove deep into the waves as the towboat and barges churned northward from Norfolk to New York.

The vessels were within sight of the Five Fathoms Lightship when the worst thing that could happen to a barge crew happened. With no notice, the Carroll became disengaged from its towboat, and was at the whim of the relentless pounding of the ocean waves. Soon after, the other barges also broke their tow.

As the towline to the Carroll went limp, a distress signal sounded from the Montrose. Her captain, A.C. Simmons, managed to maintain the integrity of the two remaining barges, but it was instantly apparent that the Carroll was in peril.

There can be no substantive testimony about the chain of events aboard the Carroll after it split from its tug. The four-man crews from the Hallowell and Hooper were rescued by Coast Guardsmen, and their barges were towed by a cutter to Cape May. The Carroll, bobbing and dipping in heavy seas, was not as fortunate. It was felt that two crewmen were almost instantly swept overboard to their deaths, but the other two somehow launched a lifeboat and attempted to save themselves.

After snaring the wayward Hallowell and Hooper, the Coast Guardsmen initiated a thorough search for the Carroll, which was last spotted about nine miles southwest of the Five Fathoms Lightship. The barge was never seen again, but after a long night of searching, the morning light shone on a grisly sight.

Shortly before 7 in the morning, Monday, February 17, 1930, the crew of Patrol Boat 218 out of Cape May sighted a small craft off the coast. Chief Boatswain's Mate John Sundfor brought his boat closer, until it was obvious that they had found the lifeboat from the Carroll.

What they looked upon was one of the most horrible and graphic examples of the sea havings its way with the men who attempt to tame it.

The very boat that was meant to carry the men of the Carroll to salvation had become their coffin. The Coast Guard crewmen looked into the well of the lifeboat and saw, still in sitting positions, the ragged corpses of F.T. Keith and Philip Frazner. Their clothing and hair bore the icy frosting of a freezing night of exposure to the elements, and their skin had discolored to the sickening blue-gray of frozen flesh and blood.

Perhaps most poignant of all, however, was the position of the men's hands. Their fear—their desperate struggle against the sea's uncompromising rage was obscenely portrayed in the way their hands, frozen in a death grip, were still curled around the oars of the lifeboat!

U-BOATS INVADE CAPE MAY

"Do you have zee papers?"

It is a common phrase used when mimicking stern, square-jawed German officers who glare at confrontees and demand proper identification or authorization.

It was a common phrase actually used by stern, square-jawed German officers during World War I, just before they took the measure of innocent American merchant ships.

In testimony from merchant captains victimized by the German U-boats that wreaked havoc with coastal shipping, it was revealed that in most of the encounters, the submarine surfaced near the freighter or tanker, ordered all hands into lifeboats, demanded "zee papers" (the ship's cargo manifest) from the captain, and with little emotion, sank the unarmed vessel.

The saga of the unterseeboots around Cape May and, indeed, in the Delaware Bay itself, during the first world war is a saga of shipwreck and legend. It borders on the incredible.

As authorities grew wary of the German incursion in 1917, many precautions were taken along the eastern seaboard to protect the nation's vital harbor cities. The port of Philadelphia was protected ever so briefly by a steel chain net strung in the Delaware River from Fort Delaware (Pea Patch Island) to the Jersey side of the river. This submarine protection lasted only from the summer 1917 to an early winter storm that swept it away later in the year.

The German submarine command believed the New Jersey shipping lanes would be ripe for the picking. Plans included destroying as much tonnage as possible, and setting mine traps in the Delaware Bay. For a brief time, those plans were carried out with great success.

Word of the actual presence of Hun subs in American waters came in May, 1918, when the American steamer "Nyanza" was ambushed by what was later presumed to be the notorious undersea raider, the U-151. The Nyanza evaded the sub's gunfire and errant torpedoes and escaped into shallow water. Later, the "Johancy" and "J.C. Donnell" encountered the sub, but also escaped unscathed.

Later, the British tanker "Cheyenne" was approached by the U-151, and even traded shots with her, before reaching the safety of the Delaware Bay.

The Cheyenne's report of the U-151's aggression sparked increased awareness of the proximity of the enemy, and opened a bizarre chapter of America's war history.

The World War I submarine action off the eastern coast of the United States lasted only a few months, and although it did hinder coastal shipping, it did not play a major role in the eventual outcome of the war.

Instead of responding to the coastal defense call by redeploying warships to the eastern seaboard, a more austere arrangement was made.

Admiral William Sims, commander of the Fourth Naval District, began preparations for the defense by ordering eight wooden fishing boats of the menhaden fleet berthed at Lewes, Delaware, to be converted into makeshift minesweepers. These vintage, wooden boats were sent to Cape May for future use. At the same time, Admiral Sims appropriated several power boats, affixed naval numbers to them and christened them as sub chasers for the bay and shore areas.

On May 25, 1918, the U-151 sank several vessels off the New Jersey coast. Under the command of the charismatic Korvetten-kapitan Von Nostitz, the sub caught each victim unaware, boarded her, planted time bombs aboard her, and aided all crewmen to safety.

Von Nostitz spoke fluent English, and was said to have been quite courteous, albeit businesslike, in his approach to the men who were then forced to watch their ship explode and sink. It was also reported that on several occasions, the German commander would apologize when explaining that he was interested in shipping tonnage, not human lives.

The German sub crew usually did pilfer what it could, for shipboard or sometimes personal use, and they did insist that the ensigns of the allied nations be stricken. There were incidents where crewmen of the victimized ships were held captive in the subs, but most reported being treated well. They said the German sailors played games, exchanged photographs, taught German, and were generally quite humane.

Still, they were the ruthless enemy. No ship—from the smallest fishing scow to the luxurious liners—was immune to the U-boats' fury.

There were only six German subs reported off the coast, but they held America's east coast in their grip for several months in 1918.

After the initial skirmishes with the Nyanza, Johancy, J.C. Donnell and Cheyenne, the U-151 prowled around and found the "Hattie Dunn," "Edna" and "Hauppauge." Each was damaged by time bombs in the aforementioned fashion and taken out of commission.

On May 28, the U-151 actually entered the Delaware Bay and planted several mines between Capes May and Henlopen. The rough currents at the bay entrance tossed the sub around so viciously, however, that Von Nostitz feared damage to his ship and ordered the sub turned around toward the calmer open sea.

Meanwhile, the Navy Department responded to random reports of sub action off the coast by vehemently denying them. There was even an attempt to censor the news, but survivors arriving on shore told of their experiences, and word-of-mouth could not be stifled. After the press disclosed the survivors' stories, the military admitted that there were German submarines just off the New Jersey beaches.

There was a curious admixture of the fear of the Hun being so close and the unusual tales of compassion coming from the survivors. The crew of one sunken freighter told of how the Germans brought them aboard, fed them, entertained them, and hailed a passing vessel so they could be rescued.

These vignettes were not to be confused with the purpose of the subs' mission. That became painfully evident on June 2, when the liner "Carolina" was sent to the bottom, while some 300 passengers and crew were sent scurrying for their lives. (NOTE: See "Shipwrecks Off Ocean City" by Seibold and Adams for details on this incident)

On the same day, the oil tanker "Herbert L. Pratt" became the first confirmed victim of a German mine off Cape May. The bow of the Pratt opened up after striking the mine, and while the radio operator was tapping out an S.O.S., the captain was attempting to make a dash for the Delaware Breakwater. The vessel nearly made it to safety, but the pumps couldn't win the battle with the incoming water, the engine room flooded and the Pratt went dead in the water. It sank off Hen and Chickens Shoal. All crew members escaped without injury, but the tanker remained very visible, with its bow resting on the bottom and its stern poking above the surface. It stood as a notice to passing vessels that the enemy was near.

As summer weather bathed the New Jersey shore with warmth and sunshine, there was much apprehension. Many vacation reservations at Cape May were cancelled as visitors chose what they hoped would be a safer place to spend their time. In place of the sun 'n' fun crowd, Cape May was nearly overrun by newspaper reporters.

The swelling ranks of newsmen at Cape May made the military authorities very nervous. The general public tended to believe the papers and discount any government denials of the increasing war action just off shore, and to ensure control of the situation, Cape May was placed under martial law on June 3, 1918 and the telephone system was seized by the government.

One by one, American schooners and steamers were gunned, mined, bombed and torpedoed as the U-151 cut a swath of maritime destruction in the vital shipping lanes. On June 2 alone, the sub accounted for 14,517 tons of ship and cargo as three sailing vessels and three steamers fell prey to the submarine. The big prize was the 5,000-ton Carolina.

After June 3, and a couple more attacks, the U-151 departed the New Jersey shore and headed south for more action. But before the sub returned to its base in Kiel, Germany on July 31, the marauder accounted for 23 sunken ships, 50,000 tons of shipping and 47 lives.

The Jersey shore was still not safely "out of the woods." Other U-boats were off the coast, and there was an ever-mounting fear that the shore itself could be attacked.

On June 3, the menhaden fishing boats-turned-minesweepers combed the Delaware Bay from cape to cape, looking for mines. They found and destroyed three mines that day, and a fourth on June 9. A fifth mine accounted for was the one that damaged the tanker, Pratt. To this day, some local divers and wreck-watchers believe there still might be some unaccounted-for mines from World War I somewhere down there.

On Cape May, suspicions mounted at a near fever pitch. The military carried out its defense strategies, and the civilians tried best to cope while seemingly on the brink of the war itself.

By mid-summer, rumors of German agents and spies coming ashore were the topic of discussion up and down the New Jersey coast. Many people, in a frenzy of either patriotism or fear, had their neighbors investigated or arrested for the slightest suspicion of aiding the enemy. Those with even the slightest German accent were the most logical targets of this wrath.

A Cape May man was arrested for allegedly sending night signals from his beach home to a submarine off shore. He was later released when it was discovered that the "signal" light was actually a defective porch light.

A woman on the cape was accused of sending coded signals to a German sub, but she explained that the "code" flags were just sheets on wash day.

In Ocean City, a man was shot and killed by a military patrol on the beach. He was suspected of signalling the enemy, but it was later revealed that the man had a history of deranged behavior and was likely trying to call attention to himself through his errant activities.

Even fishing boats that went out and came back without much of a catch were suspected of supplying the enemy with provisions and fuel. Why else, figured some Hun-shy zealots on shore, would they be coming back with an empty well?

The Fourth of July at Cape May, always a patriotic extravaganza, was particularly dazzling in 1918. Armed forces personnel arrived early to partake in the festivities, and visitors crowded into the town that was so close to the actual war. It was a glorious time to wave the American flag, and especially at Cape May.

Without warning, and with savage speed, a horrifying fire swept through the dry pine buildings of the Fourth Naval District Submarine Patrol Headquarters just outside of Cape May. Flames and smoke shot into the sky, and little could be done to douse the blaze. Most of the service personnel and base firefighters were in the town for the Independence Day parade, and only a few heroic men were left at the installation. They averted what could have been a major catastrophe by getting to the munitions and arms magazine before the fire did. They emptied the building by tossing the ammo into nearby water.

The Navy Department ruled the fire an accident. The public, wary of such government declarations, chose to believe that the incident might have been the work of German spies or sabateurs. Such charges were never upheld.

Precautions taken against enemy subs off Cape May resulted in the collision of the 1,900-ton steamship "Poseidon" and the navy ship "Sommerset" on July 31 just east of the Five Fathoms Bank Lightship. Both ships were steaming without running lights to evade detection. The precaution proved to be the undoing of the Poseidon, which sank after the collision. Six crewmen died.

A classic and embarrassing example of the panic created by the presence of the German subs took place in early August when an American merchant ship, armed against the threat of the enemy below, fired at a submarine as it rose from beneath the waves. The shots damaged the sub's deck gun and conning tower. The phantom of the deep managed to submerge and escape the attack. Soon after, it surfaced once again and this time was spotted by the U.S.S. Paul Jones, a destroyer on routine patrol. The skipper of the "tin can" had designs on being the first American sea captain to capture a German sub in American waters. He noticed the damage on the deck of the sub and ordered the destroyer to close in on the U-boat with all guns trained on it.

Excitement on the deck of the destroyer mounted as the main hatch of the submarine cranked open. An officer emerged from the hatchway, frantically waving and screaming, begging for mercy, shouting, "Don't shoot! Don't shoot! We're Americans!!"

The destroyer escorted the American submarine O-6 back to Cape May, both safe and wiser.

Other German submarines passed by Cape May and attacked other merchant ships. The big five-masted schooner "Dorothy M. Barrett" was sunk by the U-117 on August 14, and several fishing boats and merchant vessels in the immediate area sped to the scene to try to "bag" the German. The incident touched off another round of real and imagined "attacks." Any bit of flotsam became the target of gunners hoping to sink the enemy U-boat.

Other German subs continued the attacks on shipping through the summer and fall of 1918. The U-151 was replaced by others, but they found stronger American defenses. By early November, the New Jersey shore was clear of unterseeboots, and the German government and military were steadily collapsing.

On November 9, just two days before the Armistice was declared, the last victim of German sea warfare off Cape May was destroyed. The 2,500-ton army cargo ship USS Saetia, struck a mine laid by the U-117 near the Fenwick Island Lightship. The ship sank, but there were no fatalities.

Minesweeping continued at the entrance to the Delaware Bay as the victors and the vanquished signed the instruments of surrender.

On and around Cape May, everyone breathed a bit easier.

THE STRANGE CASE OF THE S-5

It is one of the most incredible stories in the history of the United States submarine service.

It is the story of a submarine that only half-submerged, went tail-up and head-down before going belly-up somewhere off the coast of Cape May.

The S-5 was on her maiden voyage from Boston to Baltimore, departing the Bay State port on Monday, August 30 for a cruise that would put the new sub through tortuous trials. Nobody on board could ever have dreamed what was to happen.

At a position described as about 55 miles off Cape Henlopen, the S-5 crew participated in yet another "crash dive" maneuver. It was the second such drill in as many days, and the previous one had been carried out without incident.

As the dive began, it became painfully obvious to those on watch that something was very, very wrong. Gunner's Mate First Class H.A. Love was in the torpedo room at the time. "After we were completely submerged," he said, "I felt water pouring into the room. I turned around quickly and saw that it was entering through the intake valve. I ran over to try to shut it. I was alone in the room. When I attempted to close the valve from the inside, I was knocked to the floor by the rush of water. I got up and tried again, and again I was bowled over. It was a powerful stream of water, but I managed to get out."

As the failed valve allowed the sea water to gush in, the sub began to sink, bow down. The weight of the eight torpedoes up front certainly contributed to the rapid descent of the bow.

Lt. Cdr. Charles M. Cooke, Jr., captain of the S-5, took immediate action, action that would later win unanimous praise from his crew. After a few minutes, as the sub faltered to a nearly vertical position, the captain led the crew through the tangled compartments. A resounding thump signalled all that the sub's bow had struck bottom. The men scrambled frantically, but in the ordered manner of submariners, from front to back in a dark and disoriented grope to the far end of the stern.

Gunner's Mate Love recalled the anxious moments: "We were forced by chlorine gas from room to room until finally we were confined in the two stern compartments, the motor room and the tiller room. We did not yet know what depths of water we were in. Before we were forced to retreat from the conning tower, we could look out and see that the bow was resting on the sand. That led us to believe that we were not in water the depth of which was more than the length of the boat."

While the flooding did begin in the forward rooms, and the descent did favor the heavier bow, the positioning of the sub in an upright fashion was not all accidental.

Chief Machinist Mate Frederick Whitehead later revealed that the cunning captain devised the unusual scheme that led to the crew's rescue.

"The captain figured out that our boat was 231 feet long and the water was but 160 feet deep and that by standing the boat on her nose the stern would project through the water's surface," said Whitehead.

The ship being longer than the water was deep, therefore, the vessel would become a virtual staircase toward salvation.

Ascending this staircase was not an easy task. To tilt the sub into the vertical position would require allowing water from other flooded compartments to find its way into the bow, and into the sensitive battery storage room. This, the crew knew, would cause potentially-dangerous chlorine gas to build up and threaten their lives.

"There was nothing else we could do," said Whitehead. "We blew out this water but as it rushed past and the stern began to rise, we were all swept along with it. Several of the men sustained injury. The salt water on the battery plates caused the formation of the chlorine gas and the men began choking."

There was a hurried search for gas masks, and most men found some. Some were forced to share the masks, and none were overcome by the fumes.

Whitehead continued his story: "The captain worked his way aft and we communicated with him through a speaking tube. We finally had to quit our post as we were choking with the gas. We got into the next compartment with difficulty and had to return to open a valve so that we could get air. The light then went out."

Gunner's Mate Love called that time after the lights went out the most frightening of all. "The worst thing we had to contend with," he said, "was the fact that we had no matches, no watches and didn't know one day from another, or when it was day or night. But every one felt that we would get out all right, as long as they could tell from the waves hitting the sides that part of the ship was out of water."

Captain Cooke and the officers maintained discipline and calm. The crew cooperated by speaking only when necessary to conserve oxygen, and remaining as still as possible to conserve energy.

The 37 men of the S-5 knew nothing of their fate. They rummaged through the ship for whatever food could be saved from the tangle of bulkheads and decks smeared with oil and water. Cans of peas, tomatoes, corned beef and beans became their meals, washed down by precious fresh water in very limited supply.

Within their tiny air bubble, temperatures soared and the air fouled. Below them, the chlorine gas was contained, but still was quite potent.

Despite the futility of it all, the men remained composed and retained their collective sense of humor. The spirit of human survival was strong, and the men kept their faith alive.

Knowing that the stern was protruding through the surface of the sea, Captain Cooke believed that a hole could somehow be punched through the sub's plates and the crew could be rescued.

There was an attempt to find enough battery power and an electric drill to facilitate that action, but all batteries were rendered useless, and the electric drill would be of no use.

They did find a small hand ratchet drill, and despite the fact that it may not have sufficed to bore through the thick shell of the sub, and it was only five-eighth of an inch wide, it was their only key to the outside.

Captain Cooke was first to take his turn with the drill. After his initial fifteen-minute session, crewmen spelled each other at about the same intervals. In pitch darkness, and with their putrid air supply dwindling, they perservered. The drill slowly and with agonizing hand labor cut through the thick steel until it pierced the sub's skin.

The light of day and a waft of fresh air surged through the compartment, and the drill—dulled and battered—was put aside. The next order as the crew continued to fight for their lives was to find a thin rod that would be pushed through the aperture.

An iron rod was found, a white undershirt was tied to it, and the makeshift distress signal was eased outside, representing a slender life line and link to the world.

One crewman reported peeking out of the hole before the rod was inserted and seeing a ship only about five miles away. The vessel apparently didn't notice the unusual sight of the S-5's stern and undershirt, and continued on its way.

Shortly after, however, through some amazing act of fate, the wooden steamer Alanthus happened upon the crippled sub and the rescue of the men of the S-5 was underway.

It must have been a bit disconcerting for the crew of the steamer when they spotted the unbelievable sight of an upright submarine in the distance. Not until they saw the waving of the distress "flag" could they have known that there was any sign of life inside the sub.

Ironically, the Alanthus itself was disabled, and was off its course. It was unprepared to undertake any serious salvage and rescue operation, but immediately its crew worked to attach a cable from the ship to the sub, and a small boat was dispatched from the Alanthus to the exposed section of the S-5.

The radio room of the Alanthus also issued a distress call, and within minutes it was received by the larger and stronger transport, General Goethals.

Shortly after the General Goethals picked up the S.O.S.,

word of the S-5's plight was beamed to shore installations and the press.

Even as details filtered through, there was more confusion and contradiction than hard fact. Initial reports to the public were inconclusive and incomplete. All that was known for certain is that the men of the S-5 were in deep peril, but still alive and rescue seemed to be just hours away.

How long the men actually spent fighting for air and life itself in their steel cell became muddled. Even in the final reports issued, the estimated time spent from sinking to salvation varied from 36 to 42 hours.

The exact details didn't really matter in the end. What mattered is that the General Goethals arrived on the scene with heavier power equipment at about 5 p.m., September 2. The Goethals, of the Panama Steamship Co. line, was on its way from Rio de Janiero to New York when it came to the aid of the S-5. By that time, the ailing sub and its escort, the Alanthus, had drifted to within about forty miles of the Five Fathoms Bank Lightship off Cape May.

Men from the General Goethals, led by Chief Engineer William R. Grace, boarded the side of the submarine and relieved those from the Alanthus who had done all they could to provide air, water and hope to the trapped submariners.

Grace and his assistant continued to drill holes through the plates of the sub until a crowbar could be used to peel back the shell wide enough to allow a man to wiggle through.

One by one, the weak and weary men from the submarine emerged. Coughing, choking, some "bleeding through the eye and nose," according to the Goethals' captain Swinton, the men were plucked from what could have become their crypt. A hastily-rigged boatswain's chair carried the men to the deck of the Alanthus, which provided soup and a bed for each of the harried victims.

After a period of rest and recuperation aboard the steamer, the men were transferred to the USS Biddle, one of several military ships (including the battleship USS Ohio) which had arrived on the scene. The Biddle, in turn, transported the men to the Philadelphia Navy Yard.

The problems faced by the crew of the S-5 were unique to submarine rescue at the time. Normally, the amount of breathing air inside the sub would be sufficient for about 72 hours, but the S-5's position (determined to be at about a 60-degree angle) altered that. Usually, the men could have attempted an escape through the torpedo tubes, but they were deep under water and inaccessible.

All that stood between certain death and survival was the quick thinking of the captain and the endurance of the crew, as well as the presence of the Alanthus and General Goethals.

Thus, when it was time to assess the situation in retrospect, there were many heroes. From Captain Swinton of the General Goethals' perspective, "all credit belonged to Chief Engineer Grace and his assistant McWilliams. If ever men were heroes," the captain said, "they were."

Captain Cooke of the S-5 felt that his crewmen themselves were the heroes. He sent a telegram to President Woodrow Wilson asking for a special commendation for each man and said, "The men fought like heroes for their freedom and their lives."

To the men of the S-5, it was their captain who emerged heroically. The men each signed a telegram to the Secretary of the Navy asking to be put right back on the S-5 after it was salvaged, with Captain Cooke as its master. If it was not salvaged, then they wanted to be stationed on any other ship to which Cooke was assigned. As Seaman Apprentice Joe Youker said, "I want to be in on the next dive and I want to make it with 'Savvy Cooke!' "

The men were landed safely at Philadelphia on September 4, and they greeted waiting reporters and civilians with broad smiles of relief. Some locked arms and sang, in jest, "How Dry I Am." Others, just happy to be alive, flashed grins and sought their own kind of peace.

There was one common request from each of the men. Each and every crewman desired just one thing. After spending nearly two days in thin, sickening air, after having all their strength sapped from them by choking and gagging from the wisp of chlorine-laced oxygen, they all had but one request upon reaching dry land and clear air. Each of them asked for . . . a cigarette!

The inquiry as to what exactly happened to the S-5 was conducted first aboard the battleship Ohio. It was determined that a faulty valve resulted in the accident. The submarine itself was being towed inland when, just off Cape May, it broke tow and sank back to the bottom of the sea in one last act of defiance.

THE CAPE BRACES FOR ANOTHER WAR

During the first world war, Karl Doenitz sailed as an officer in the Kaiser's submarine fleet. By the end of the second world-wide conflict, he had risen through the ranks to become commander of the entire Nazi navy and, upon the death of Adolf Hitler, the leader of the crumbled German nation.

Perhaps his knowledge of America's unpreparedness in World War I prompted him to send subs once again to the eastern seaboard of the United States in 1942.

Most of the Nazi underwater warships were operating in the Arctic and North Atlantic oceans in early 1942, intercepting Allied shipping headed for Russia. But the top Nazi naval brass hankered for the relatively unprotected and very tempting eastern U.S. shore.

The U-boats were racking up impressive kills up north. Some 14,000 tons of shipping went down in April, 1942 and that figure nearly doubled the next month. Vice-Admiral Friedrich Ruge, however, set his sights to the American shore. "Had those submarines in the Arctic been off the American coast," he wrote after the war, "they would have scored five to ten times that much."

Admiral Doenitz, in his memoirs, noted, "There were, admittedly, anti-submarine patrols, but they were wholly lacking in experience. Single destroyers, for example, sailed up and down the traffic lanes with such regularity that the U-boats were quickly able to work out the time-table being followed."

In retrospect, the eastern seaboard's defenses were almost laughable, in a tragic sense of the word.

Coastal resort lights spread across the horizon like an illuminated string of pearls, or, for the Nazi U-boats' purposes, like so many beacons lighting the backdrop for attack.

The U-boats came to the coastline in the dead of winter. There were only six to eight of them, but they made the most of the pathetic situation in the eastern shipping lanes. In February, 1942, alone, the submarines' devastating darts of death and destruction accounted for 30 sinkings and 166,000 tons of shipping lost.

The massive concrete bunker that stands at the very point of Cape May once housed several powerful guns designed to protect the entrance of the Delaware Bay from any enemy aggression. It, and other bunkers deep in the dunes of Cape Henlopen across the bay, are massive, stark and silent reminders of those anxious months and years.

Likewise, the fire control towers used to support the bunkers, stand as strange monuments to the World War II era.

What is not seen, however, are reminders of less substantial coastal protection attempts. As threatening as the Cape May Point bunker may look, these other defensive measures seem tame and almost medieval. In their own ways, though, they were vital.

Civilians on the cape had to know what was going on just beyond their vision out at sea. Loud blasts, rattling dishes and windows marked the end of another merchant vessel somewhere out there, although there was no word in the press about it for several days, if ever. Oil slicks and wreckage washed up on shore, but the military authorities were reluctant to confirm the "kill."

On the beaches, the Coast Guard's Beach Patrol, known as "Beach Pounders," were on duty, keeping watch on horseback and with watch dogs at their side.

About two thousand dogs were pressed into patrol duty in the "Dogs for Defense" program in 1942. The pooch patrol started at Brigantine, New Jersey, and the dogs were trained at a compound in suburban Philadelphia.

Within a year, the canine ranks almost doubled, and the beaches of Cape May were patrolled regularly by dogs, horses and the humans of the Temporary Reserve units of the Coast Guard.

It may be difficult to consider a defense made up of horses, dogs and volunteers in a war during which the Germans were making rockets and the Americans were perfecting the atomic bomb. Still, for their time, their place, and their purpose, the crude patrols were adequate.

Still, there are persistent rumors that some Germans penetrated the defense efforts on the beach and infiltrated American society and its government. There are also those who claim to know for certain that a Nazi submarine was actually destroyed just off Cape May in shallow water and its remains are still there, for whatever diver may find them.

THE END OF THE "JAKIE"

Dateline: February 27, 1942.

There was no warning.

The Nazi torpedo ripped through the steel shell of the vintage American destroyer like a hot knife through butter. With an excrutiating blast, dozens of men were killed. That single shot from the U-boat marked the beginning of the end for the USS Jacob Jones.

In a flash of fire and shredded steel, the ship's captain, executive officer and scores of enlisted men were slaughtered. The seconds ticked off, and in another instant another underwater bullet crashed through the stern section of the Jones. More men died, and others were shaken into the stark reality of war.

The action was not in the North Sea, the Meditteranean, or the open Atlantic. The U-578, a newly-built German pigboat, had been sent by Admiral Karl Doenitz into the busy coastal shipping lanes of the United States of America. The United States was caught with its maritime pants down.

Already, in other parts of the world, U.S. ships like the Salinas, Kearny and Reuben Jones were listed among the casualties of war. Since the capture of the City of Flint by the Germans in 1939, America was all too aware of the might and daring of the Nazi navy.

Defense of the eastern coastline was beginning to take shape. Patrol boats were being deployed to protect shipping and, ultimately, the coast itself.

So sensitive and gunshy were the coastal patrols that their actions took on Keystone Kops appearances at times. It was well known that trigger-happy gunners had shot and and destroyed numerous buoys, rocks and bits of flotsam, believing the shadowy figures in the water to be submarine sails. Whales were especially deceiving targets.

Near hysteria swept the coastal defenses when, in January, 1942, U.S. Army reconnaisance planes spotted six mysterious ships off Cape May and radioed back that a German "invasion fleet" was on its way. The invaders turned out to be common fishing trawlers.

But with World War II at the nation's doorstep, no precautions were too stringent. The Jacob Jones was one of several World War I—era destroyers pressed into service for coastal duty. Its lookouts were to maintain a sharp vigil along her appointed course, just beyond the horizon from Cape May.

To her 140 crewmen, she was the "Jakie." To naval historians, she was the reincarnation of another USS Jacob Jones that, in tragic irony, was the victim of a German unterseeboot on December 6, 1917.

Less than a year after that sinking, a new "tin can" slipped into the Delaware River after her launching in Camden on Armistice Day, 1918. She would be the latest vessel to carry the name of Jones, a War of 1812 battle hero.

The 314-foot destroyer could do 35 knots through the water and was armed with a dozen torpedo tubes, four four-inch guns and a pair of depth charge racks.

On the last day of the Jakie, her skipper, Lt. Cdr. Hugh Black, a 38-year old academy man considered to be an up-and-coming officer, was running a particularly tight ship. Already, he and his men had tasted war.

Not two weeks prior, the Jacob Jones was steaming off the Virginia capes when it discovered a lifeboat filled with men who appeared to be on the verge of death. After rescuing them, it was discovered that they were part of the crew of the Buarque, a Brazilian passenger-cargo ship that had been torpedoed off Cape Hatteras some 60 hours before! The survivors spent those hours—40 of which were in a driving rain storm—on the lifeboat. They were given safe haven aboard the Jacob Jones.

Another incident was especially fresh in the Jakie's crew's

mind. As they passed the northern New Jersey coastline on their way from New York harbor to their post off Cape May, they came close by the hulk of the R.P. Resor, an Esso Oil tanker that had been ripped by Nazi torpedoes on February 26, 1942.

The horrid picture of black smoke and smoldering steel became all too real the very next day as the "Jakie" and all but eleven of her men met their fates.

Joe Tidwell, a 22-year old Alabaman, recalled the morning's events. "I had just gone up to the galley to get some sugar for some coffee we had made when there was a terrible explosion forward and the ship seemed to bog down," he told reporters after the incident. Tidwell, who was on watch in the aft engine room, said the explosion took place at about five minutes before five in the morning.

"Pots and pans in the galley began to rain down over our heads, and then there was another explosion," he continued. "I ran up to see what had happened and found some of the boys cutting rafts away. I jumped in the water and climbed on one raft with two other men."

Tidwell said he could actually make out the silhouette of a submarine about a hundred yards off the port beam of the Jones.

The second torpedo blast, the one that struck the after section of the destroyer, also touched off several depth charges on the Jones' fantail.

This series of explosions killed more men who were trying desperately to reach life rafts or cling to wreckage that floated in the oily water.

The bow and stern sections of the ship were devastated by the torpedos, but somehow the entire midships compartment remained afloat for several minutes.

Due to that fact, amid the tales of tragedy and death, there were tidbits that border on the comic relief. "I wasn't going out in that cold water without getting something warm in my stomach," related Kentuckian Tom Moody, who told of how he took a final swig of coffee and raided a long-underwear locker to bundle up. "That's a nice thing about the Navy," he said, "you get plenty of heavy underwear!"

All around Moody and the fortunate ones in the mid-section,

there was mayhem. More and more explosions ensued as the depth charges were ignited. With each blast, more men perished. "They just died . . . one at a time . . . that's all," said one survivor.

Joe Tidwell told investigators later that the survivors were "a very orderly bunch." He and others did what they could to supply as many makeshift rafts and flotation devices as possible. "The front end of what was left of the ship was sunk under, and Richard Dors climbed back up on the middle section to see if he could cut another raft loose and maybe help some of the other fellows off the boat," Tidwell recalled. Dors, of Brockton, Massachusetts, said the effort proved futile. "When my feet got wet, I jumped in the water again and swam for a while," he said. "When I reached another raft with some other fellows on it I grabbed a hold, then looked around and saw the last of the 'Jakie' go down. I was still holding on when a big explosion knocked some of the fellows off of their rafts and almost blew me out of the water, but I held on. The water was plenty cold, about 38 degrees. About four hours later, we were picked up."

They were picked up and taken to Cape May, where the nine petty officers and two apprentice seamen told their stories.

Those eleven fortunate sailors might have derived some modicum of satisfaction from news that broke later in the war. They would eventually find out that the U-578, which claimed responsibility for the sinking of the Jakie, was itself sunk in battle in August, 1942. And, the Jakie's sister ship, the USS Roper, went on to track down and kill the U-85, another Nazi sub which had chalked up many kills in the Atlantic.

These tidbits could not have provided much solace for the eleven survivors of the Jakie incident, but the sinking of the destroyer did provide a stimulus for the Navy Department to begin to report the sinking of U.S. ships by the enemy along the eastern shore. Although about 30 ships were sunk by the Nazis in February, 1942, close-in along the coast, the public knew very little. Unfortunately, until the coastal protection could be beefed up, more ships and more men would be claimed by the bold German U-boats.

Today, all that remains of the Jakie are two chunks of wreckage on the sea floor. The bow section is in 110 feet of water, about 24 miles from Cape May Inlet on a 145-degree heading. Another piece of the ship is about six miles farther out, in deeper water.

FISHERMAN'S DREAM/ FISHERMAN'S NIGHTMARE

Thousands perish as boats capsize off Townsend Inlet!!

Sure, it's stretching things a bit, but it is entirely accurate.

The 28-foot fishing boat Antoinette and the 32-foot San Sennero enjoyed a full day of work on April 27, 1944, and their holds proved it.

The Antoinette was nearly bursting with an estimated 5,000 pounds of mackeral, while the San Sennero was loaded with about 3,000 pounds of the sea's harvest.

In cruel irony, the abundance from the depths proved to be the undoing of the two vessels. As they approached the shallows just off Avalon, the tons of fish got the best of them. To the amazement of both crews, both ships began to list and founder, and in an instant, both capsized!

A Coast Guard crew responded, and the five fishermen, and eventually their vessels, were saved.

THE LOSS OF THE WOOLWORTH YACHT

The war was still raging on January 6, 1944, but somehow it seemed so very far away.

The German submarines that had for so long terrorized United States coastal shipping, had left the area a year before. After claiming hundreds of ships, hundreds of lives and hundreds of thousands in tonnage, the U-boats simply ran out of fuel and torpedoes and were deployed to other hunting grounds.

The fact that America had effectively beefed-up its coastal defenses also contributed to the sudden disappearance of the Nazi subs, so that strong U.S. military presence along the coast continued.

One of the small but potent warships that was part of the Eastern Sea Frontier patrol activity, also known as the "bucket brigade" along the east coast, was a Navy patrol boat with a thoroughbred blood line.

She was, for Navy purposes, the St. Augustine, PG-54. Her decks bristled with armament and she was built for speed. She was manned by 145 sailors, and had to be one of the classiest hulls in the fleet.

Before her homely coat of Navy gray, she was resplendent in her best seagoing bib-and-tucker as the floating toy of the incredibly rich and storied Woolworth family of New York City.

The 272-foot, 1,300-ton vessel was built in Newport News, Virginia, in 1929 for George F. Baker, Jr. at a cost of $1,250,000. Christened as the "Viking," the ship was later purchased by Norman Woolworth and re-named the "Noparo."

In December, 1940, the Navy bought the ship at a "bargain basement" price of $180,000, refitted her at the Boston Navy Yard and gave her the new name, "St. Augustine."

But even this noble lineage couldn't save the converted pleasure boat from a horrible fate.

For more than a year after her commissioning, the gunboat spent a routine tour of duty out of Boston Harbor. As the German submarines began to assert themselves up and down the eastern seaboard in 1942, the St. Augustine was sent south to escort merchant convoys bound from New York to ports in the Caribbean.

On January 6, 1944, the sea some sixty miles southwest of Cape May was relatively calm. The night was cold and clear, and a steady, strong wind was blowing. It was hardly the kind of vile weather normally associated with sea tragedies.

On shore and within the shipping lanes, a "dimout" was still in effect. The St. Augustine, on routine escort duty toward Guantanamo Bay, Cuba, was sailing with only the barest minimum of lighting.

So, too, was the big freighter Camas Meadows, an American merchant tanker.

These two ships were not destined to pass in the night. The winds turned gusty and unpredictable, and the small gunboat rose and settled into the building waves. After it was too late, the helmsman of the giant tanker noticed the smaller patrol boat directly in his path. A collision could not be prevented.

The bow of the tanker tore the former yacht apart as it crashed into it with a savage, mangling crunch. The seams of the St. Augustine split open, sea water gushed in, and scores of crewmen below decks were swept away.

There was no warning. There was no time to abandon ship. Within minutes, the St. Augustine was swirling to the bottom.

It was 11:30 at night, and the Camas Meadows immediately sent out an S.O.S. Rescue ships and boats from Cape May sped to the scene, but found the worst.

Several bodies were recovered, many never were. When all was said and done, thirty survivors were plucked from the icy sea. They were taken to the Coast Guard facility in Cape May, as were the corpses of the others. When the final muster was taken, it was revealed that 115 sailors had died.

Indeed, the war seemed so far away on January 6, 1944. But the spectre of the conflict and its widespread ramifications had reared its ugly head just off the coast of Cape May.

HULK OF A DEATH SHIP

This is the story of a ship that died twice. It is the story of the ship that burned in an incident that is the worst maritime disaster in the United States during the twentieth century.

The paddle-wheel steamer "General Slocum" was built in 1891 as an excursion boat and was put into service on the busy and profitable waterways that weave through and around New York City.

From the start, the vessel was not among the most respected in the East and Hudson Rivers. It compiled a long list of accidents, groundings and collisions, and was well-known as a ship devoid of most common safety equipment. It was marginally maintained and regarded by many in the trade as the proverbial accident waiting to happen.

That accident took place June 15, 1904 in the East River. Hundreds of happy folks from St. Mark's German Lutheran Church in the Bronx were aboard for their annual outing. As the General Slocum cruised the narrow passage between the boroughs, a passing tugboat noticed smoke billowing from the steamer's deck. The master of the tug signalled the bridge of the Slocum, but no immediate action was taken by the steamer.

Within minutes, though, the captain of the Slocum realized something was wrong. The river shorelines were only hundreds of feet away, but Capt. W.H. Van Schaick opted to continue sailing downstream, hoping to ground the Slocum on an island.

The fire on board spread quickly, but not as quickly as the panic among the passengers.

Scores leaped from the high deck of the Slocum, only to die in the water. Others were overcome by smoke or burned to death. When the Slocum finally did beach and the damage was assessed, more than 1,000 corpses were gathered.

The Slocum's captain was convicted of criminal negligence, and the 264-foot hulk of the death ship lay abandoned.

Obviously, this story does not qualify as a "shipwreck 'round Cape May." The local connection was made several years later, after the steel ship was salvaged, its superstructure scrapped, and the hollowed-out hull converted for use as a barge.

Ocean City scuba diver Ed Michaud details the second death and the rotting remains of the General Slocum, a steamer converted to a barge and renamed "Maryland."

"She was in about fifteen feet of water after she burned," he says. "They salvaged what they could from the wreckage and gutted her. She was re-bought from the underwriters, and became a coal hauler. She went up and down the coast for a number of years as the barge, Maryland.

"She was being towed north toward New York with a load of coal. At about Sea Isle City, she began to founder. They had to cut her loose, she had a leak. There was a slight northeaster at the time. It was rough water, probably going over her railings, so they cut her loose and just let her drift. They couldn't take the chance of towing her and going down with her."

Michaud claims the wreck is well known and easily accessible for divers. "She's been dove on for many years, but most people don't know what she was. Today all that exists are a few ribs and a few steel plates, some old steam fittings and things like that. There are some big quarter-inch plates down there. It's between Whale Beach and Corson's Inlet, about 1,500 feet out in about twenty feet of water. You can't miss it. She covers and uncovers, depending on the shift of the sand. Some days you don't see much, others days you can really see her plates.

"There's still coal on her. You can go out there and get all the anthracite you want. If the price of coal ever goes up, it may be worthwhile salvaging."

For those visitors to Whale Beach, near Sea Isle City, it might be worth noting that any stray pieces of coal that might ever wash up on shore might be more than a mere curiosity. They might by chunks of coal from within the belly of the death ship—the ship that took more than 1,000 human lives, burned, was given a second life and then died again, 'round Cape May!

OTHER SHIPWRECKS 'ROUND CAPE MAY

1855

April 6   *GOLDEN WEST, schooner, en route from Boston to Philadelphia with a cargo of foodstuffs, saved near Townsend Inlet*

1860

April 3   *HANNAH GRANT, schooner, bound from Portland, Me. to Philadelphia with foodstuffs, saved near Townsend Inlet*

1862

Jan. 31   *PROWESS, schooner, en route from New York to Baltimore, lost off Townsend Inlet, crew saved*

1863

Jan. 24   *MORTIMER LIVINGSTON, ship, headed to New York from Le Havre, France. Foundered on Ludlam's Beach. Two died while saving 300 other passengers. Ship as a total loss.*

April 3	MARY AND SUSAN, brig, bound from Philadelphia to New Bedford, Mass., saved off Townsend Inlet
Nov. 21	DAVID DUFFEL, brig, from Boston to Philadelphia in ballast, saved on Townsend Inlet bar

1864

Feb. 20	WAVE, brig, in ballast, lost at Hereford Inlet

1865

Jan. 8	ELIZA POTTER, schooner, from Port Royal to New York with a cargo of rags and wood, saved on Ludlam's Beach
Jan. 20	RICHARD THOMPSON, schooner, saved on Ludlam's Beach
June 8	ADMIRAL DuPONT, collided with STADACONA off Cape May with 18 fatalities
Aug. 20	COLORADO, schooner, from Philadelphia to New York with a cargo of coal, lost Townsend Inlet
Aug. 30	E.G. WILLARD, schooner, from Philadelphia to Portland, Me. with a load of coal, saved on Seven Mile Beach
Nov. 28	W.C. DEWALL, schooner, Georgetown, D.C., to Boston, lost on Seven Mile Beach
Nov. 29	E.S. CONANT, schooner, Boston to Philadelphia with lumber, saved at Townsend Inlet
Dec. 3	CARTHAGNA, schooner, saved just north of Turtle Gut Inlet

1866

Feb. 16	MARY HALEY, schooner from New York to Philadelphia, saved at Townsend Inlet

Mar. 6	WILLIAM PAXTON, schooner, bound from New York to Texas, saved off Townsend Inlet
Mar. 6	PALMETTO STATE, schooner from New York to Norfolk, lost off Cape May
Mar. 24	ALBEMARLE, schooner from Boston to Philadelphia in ballast, a total loss on Seven Mile Beach
May 20	ADDIE HARRIS, schooner from New York to Philadelphia with a load of gravel, lost on Ludlam Beach

1867

Nov. 15	SOLOMON WASHBURN, schooner, from New York to Philadelphia, saved on Seven Mile Beach
Nov. 20	MERRIMAC, ship, from Liverpool, England, to Philadelphia, cargo saved but ship a total loss on Seven Mile Beach
Dec. 15	F.R. BAIRD, schooner, in ballast, saved at Townsend Inlet

1868

Jan. 2	N. JONES, headed to Norfolk from New York, saved near Townsend Inlet
Feb. 6	ANN TURNER, schooner, bound from New York to Wilmington, N.C., saved off Cape May
March 20	ALICE M. RIDGWAY, schooner out of Tuckerton, N.J., bound from Cape May to Philadelphia with a load of gravel. The ship was overturned in a severe nor'easter snowstorm. Captain Thomas McKean Jr. and three others all died, but the vessel was discovered belly-up, salvaged and refitted. The same ship grounded on Cold Springs Bar on February 14, 1877, but all crewmen and the ship were saved
April 5	SARAH A. GREEN, schooner, crew saved but ship lost at Ludlam's Beach

April 12	SILVER LAKE, schooner, bound from New York to Philadelphia with a cargo of salt, lost at Hereford Inlet
Aug. 3	JOHN THOMPSON, bound from Portland, Me., to Philadelphia, lost at Hereford Inlet
Aug. 12	PHILANDER ARMSTRONG, schooner, lost at Hereford Inlet
Oct. 22	ST. JAGO, barkentine, in ballast, lost near Townsend Inlet
Oct. 23	E.W. GARDNER, schooner, Boston to Philadelphia, lost near Townsend Inlet
Dec. 21	ELECTRIC, ship, bound from Hamburg, Germany to New York, ship and 363 passengers saved off Cape May
Dec. 22	BELLE, schooner, snagged bottom wreckage near Townsend Inlet, capsized, but eventually saved

1869

Dec. 5	R.W. DILLON, schooner loaded with coal, lost near Townsend Inlet
Dec. 5	WILLIE MOWE, schooner, with a cargo of fish, saved off Townsend Inlet

1870

Jan. 18	SHETUCKET, ship, bound from Philadelphia to New York, loaded with coal and manure, crew saved but vessel lost off Cape May
Dec. 20	HULDAY, barkentine, loaded with chalk, lost on Seven Mile Beach

1871

Jan. 20	ARIES, steamship, bound from Boston to Philadel-

phia with a general cargo. Three men died when ship capsized on Hereford Bar

1872

Jan. 14   MARY E. COYEN, *schooner, bound from New York to Philadelphia with a cargo of barley, saved on Cold Spring Bar*

Oct. 26   LEIHA BARKARKER, *brig out of Austria, bound from Rio de Janiero to New York with coffee, saved on Cape May*

Oct. 30   MARIETTE, *schooner, from Boston to Philadelphia with her holds filled with fish, saved on Cold Spring Bar*

Nov. 26   L.S. LEVERING, *from Providence, R.I. to Philadelphia, saved off Cape May*

Dec. 23   CARRIE S. WEBB, *schooner, foundered off Turtle Gut Bar, crew found to be frostbitten, but treated and ship was saved*

Dec. 23   SILVER SPRAY, *sloop loaded with oysters, foundered on Cape May*

Dec. 23   B.F. REEVES, *schooner, from New York to the Maurice River, grounded on Cape May*

1873

Mar. 20   CLARA DAVIDSON, *schooner loaded with shingles, saved on Cape May.*

Oct. 27   MARY C. SIMMONS, *schooner, to Philadelphia in ballast, saved at Townsend Inlet*

Nov. 20   TRADEWIND, *schooner, Providence to Philadelphia in ballast, saved at Townsend Inlet*

Dec. 7   FLORENCE, *schooner, saved at Cold Spring Bar*

1874

April 4   GENERAL SHERIDAN, schooner, loaded with oysters, saved at Cold Spring Bar

Nov. 25   RICARD BARROS, schooner out of Spain, bound from Havana to New York with oranges, saved at Hereford Inlet

Dec. 11   G.M. PARTRIDGE, schooner bound from Baltimore to Belfast, Northern Ireland with corn, foundered at Cold Spring Inlet

Dec. 15   SARAH J. BRIGHT, schooner in ballast, saved at Townsend Inlet

1875

March 8   L & A BABCOCK, schooner bound from Philadelphia to Boston in ballast, saved at Tonwsend Inlet

March 15   EVALINE, sloop, saved at Townsend Inlet

March 27   EARLY BIRD, sloop, bound from New York to St. Augustine, Florida, saved at Townsend Inlet

April 24   WORDEN & EVANS, schooner, in ballast, saved off Cape May

April 24   N.C. PRICE, sloop, saved off Cape May

Oct. 4   CHINA, schooner, bound from Bangor, Me. to Charleston, S.C. with a general cargo, lost on Ludlam Beach.

Nov. 18   C.R. PRICE, schooner loaded with oysters, lost on Cold Spring Bar

Nov. 27   MARY FREELAND, schooner, bound from Boston to Philadelphia, saved on Poverty Beach

1876

Feb. 3   HANNAH, bark, loaded with coal oil, one fatality and ship lost off Cape May

May 8   EMALINE McLAIN, bound from Boston to Philadel-

	phia with a cargo of stones, lost at Townsend Inlet
June 21	ELLA, schooner bound from San Juan, P.R. to New York with sugar and mollases, saved at Hereford Inlet
Sept. 17	THOMAS J. LANCASTER, schooner bound from Boston to Philadelphia with ice, saved on Ludlam Beach
Nov. 20	WHITE FOAM, schooner bound from Providence to Baltimore in ballast, saved on Townsend Inlet bar

1877

Feb. 28	CORINNE, a 58-ton vessel built in 1864, struck bottom off Cape May and was a total loss
Feb. 28	E.S. NEWMAN, schooner, bound from the Caribbean to New York with sugar, saved on Cape May
March 9	BETHANY, bark out of Australia; a cargo of tea, silks and china valued at $600,000. Part of the cargo was saved, 11 crewmen survived, but the ship was a total loss.
March 12	FRANK B. COLTON, schooner, bound from Boston to Philadelphia in ballast, saved at Turtle Gut Bar
March 15	TWILIGHT, schooner loaded with coal, saved on Cold Spring Bar
March 28	ADDIE SCHAEFER, schooner, bound from Norfolk to New York, saved on Cape May
March 29	YULETTE KENYON, schooner loaded with manure, saved at Townsend Inlet
May 8	CORDORA, schooner bound from Philadelphia to Bristol, England, with coal, lost off Cape May
June 21	ONWARD, schooner, bound from Providence to Philadelphia with flour, lost at Hereford Inlet

1882

Feb. 28	GOLDSBORO, steamship. A new steamer, she

*stranded on Brandywine Shoals and was later freed
with much damage to the hull*

1886

Nov. 17 *HIPPODROME, a steam vessel converted to coal
barge, the 24-year old craft was loaded with coal
when it was stranded on Cape May and lost*

1888

March 12 *ALLIE E. BELDEN, sank in Delaware Bay*
March 31 *WAVE CREST, schooner, foundered off Hereford Inlet*
Oct. 21 *SALLIE MORTON, schooner, bound from Millville
to New York with glass sand, sprang a leak about a
half-mile off Cape May. The crew and Captain
Thomas Shaw were rescued from the rigging, but the
20-year old ship sank in five fathoms of water with a
loss estimated at $2,000*

1889

March 27 *RUTH DARLING, schooner, collided with another
vessel off Five Fathoms Bank*

1890

Oct. 7 *H.W. GODFREY, schooner, stranded on Hereford
Inlet Bar*

1891

Jan. 11	ALSENHORN, schooner, lost in Delaware Bay
Feb. 1	JUNE BRIGHT, schooner, the 83-ton vessel was stranded on the Brandywine Shoals
April 28	WILLIAM B. ORR, sank in Delaware Bay
July 28	ARCHER AND REEVES, schooner, sank at Brandywine Shoals

1903

Jan. 30	NORTH CAROLINA, 600-ton, steel-hulled steamship, stranded at Hereford Inlet

1906

Sept. 15	VIRGINIA H. HUDSON, schooner, the 579-ton vessel, built in 1871, foundered off Hereford Inlet

1907

Jan. 25	SAMUEL H. SHARP, 236-ton schooner stranded on Cape May

1914

June 16	HANNAH A. LENNEN, steamship, collided with another vessel at entrance Delaware Bay

1915

May 8	FANNIE H. STEWART, schooner, the 33-year old

ship foundered off Cape May

Nov. 11   *F.A. ALLEN, schooner built in 1872, sank in Delaware Bay*

1918

March 10   *HAMPSHIRE, schooner, foundered east of the Five Fathom Lightship, all four hands aboard the 18-year old ship were drowned*

June 2   *CAROLINA, passenger liner, sank by German submarine U-151. See "Shipwrecks Off Ocean City" by Seibold and Adams for details*

Aug. 14   *DORIS B. BARRETT, schooner, sank off Cape May*

1923

July 25   *SAMUEL H. HARTMAN, schooner built in 1891, foundered in the Delaware Bay*

1927

Oct. 2   *BAY RIDGE, barge, sank near Cape May Inlet in 50 feet of water*

1929

April 3   *GOVERNOR ROSS, schooner, grounded on a sandbar a mile from Cape May Inlet. The boat, out of Gloucester, Mass., was the first of 150 vessels to arrive at Cape May in the annual race between mackeral fishing fleets from Gloucester to Cape May. Under full sail, the Governor Ross ventured just outside the channel and struck the bar. It later broke up on a jetty. The crew members were saved by Coast Guards and despite the mishap, the Governor Ross was declared the winner of the race*

1932

Dec. 20   *NAY AUG, schooner barge built in 1890, foundered on Seven Mile Beach*

1935

Jan. 25   *OCTORARO, barge, sank in Delaware Bay*

1936

Sept. 4   *CLARELLA, yacht, built in 1929, burned off Cape May*

1937

Sept. 22   *F.A. BECKWORTH, steamship, the 196-ton vessel built in 1904 collided with another ship and foundered four miles south of Cape May*

1939

Feb. 4   *LONNIE B. SHAW, tug, sank in a heavy storm off Cape May. The tug was pulling the barge Ruth Shaw, loaded with lumber, from New York to Virginia. The storm separated the tug from her barge, and the tug went to the bottom with a loss of seven crewmen*

1941

May 7   *FREEHOLD, steam vessel of 220 tons, built in 1903, sank near Overfalls Shoal*

1942

Feb. 5   *CHINA ARROW, sank in Delaware Bay*
May 15   *TRANSMARINE, barge, sank near Cold Spring Inlet jetty*

1945

Dec. 15   *SHANNON, sank 45 miles southeast of Cape May*

1948

Sept. 20   *EDITH, lighter, sank a mile off Cold Spring Inlet*

1949

April 1   *SALVATORE, burned in the sea southeast of Cape May*

1956

Sept. 7   *BARGE 110, barge, broke tow and sank near Cold Spring Inlet*

1957

November   DEBBIE SUE, offshore trawler, sank off Cape May,
two lives lost

1966

March 26   PHOENIX, steamship, foundered off Cape May

1967

April 27   MOCKINGBIRD, sank east of Cape May

ABOUT THE AUTHORS

David J. Seibold, of Wyomissing Hills, Pa., and Barnegat Light, N.J., is an avid boater, fisherman and diver. He is a former commodore of the Rajah Temple Yacht Club of Reading, Pa., and is a member of the Reading and Barnegat Light Scuba and Rescue Teams.

Seibold is a graduate of Pennsylvania State University and served as a company commander in the Viet Nam campaign after being commissioned in the U.S. Army Signal Corps.

An active Rotarian and member of several other civic and social organizations, Seibold is employed as an account executive at radio station WEEU in Reading, Pa.

Charles J. Adams III, of Reading, is an air personality at WEEU radio, and is also a travel and entertainment writer for the Reading Eagle newspaper. A U.S. Navy veteran, Adams serves on the board of directors of the Pennsylvania State University Alumni Society of the Berks Campus and is a school director in the Exeter Township (Pa.) School District.

Adams is also president of the board of trustees of the Reading Public Library and serves on the executive council and editorial board of the Historical Society of Berks County.

Adams has written "Ghost Stories of Berks County, Volumes I and II," and has teamed with Seibold to write "Shipwrecks Near Barnegat Inlet," "Legends of Long Beach Island" and "Shipwrecks Off Ocean City."

ABOUT THE ARTIST

The original artwork in this book is the achievement of Linda Perno Dotter, who created the pen-and-ink drawings especially for "Shipwrecks and Legends 'round Cape May."

Mrs. Dotter is a native of Long Branch, N.J., and today divides her time in Freehold and Barnegat Light, N.J., with her husband, Joseph, and four children.

She attended the Newark School of Fine and Industrial Arts, and has done numerous freelance art pieces for various firms and organizations. Her work is also exhibited frequently in art shows in northern New Jersey.

Her endeavors also graced the pages of Seibold and Adams' last book, "Shipwrecks Off Ocean City."

PHOTO GALLERY

The path to Higbee Beach leads through cedar hummocks where pirates may have buried their treasure. (Photo by Charles J. Adams III)

The transport ship SS Atlantus, one of a dozen concrete ships built during World War I, is depicted in this artist's conception.

The SS Atlantus, sunk just off Sunset Beach, was still quite visible in this 1930s post card view.

Sunset on Sunset Beach, with the remains of the wreck of the SS Atlantus silhouetted in the water while beachcombers search for "Cape May Diamonds." (Photo by Charles J. Adams III)

Co-author David J. Seibold (right) and Sunset Beach gift shop owner Marvin Hume examine railings that came from the wreck of the SS Atlantus. They are now a part of storage sheds that are to the rear of Hume's gift shop. (Photo by Charles J. Adams III)

A plaque tells the story of the remains of what is believed to be the British sloop, H.M.S. Martin, now under a pavilion in Cape May Point (Photo by Charles J. Adams III)

The weathered wooden ribs of the H.M.S. Martin can be seen at the corner of Lighthouse and Coral Avenues in Cape May Point. (Photo by Charles J. Adams III)

The Overfalls Light Ship, which once stood guard at the entrance to the Delaware Bay off Cape May, is now quietly awaiting restoration at a slip in Lewes, Delaware. (Photo by Charles J. Adams III)

Thomas Maddox, left, and Thomas Camp, experienced Jersey shore divers, look over relics retrieved from the holds of the so-called "china wreck" off Cape May. (Photo by Charles J. Adams III)

The USS Jacob Jones, sunk by a Nazi submarine in 1942, is seen in Jacksonville, Florida, in this 1937 photograph. (Photo from the collection of the Steamship Historical Society, University of Baltimore Library)

The "hoodoo ship" Northern Pacific, was beset with problems, and finally sank off Cape May in 1922 after a raging fire on board. (Photo courtesy of the Steamship Historical Society)

The Clyde Lines' pride, the liner Mohawk, was consumed by fire in January, 1925, off Cape May. (Photo courtesy of the Steamship Historical Society)

#43.

The Lenape, another Clyde Lines ship, burned off Cape May in late 1925. (Photo courtesy of the Steamship Historical Society)

Looming over the surf like a concrete monster, this bunker housed massive guns designed to guard the entrance to the Delaware Bay during World War II. It is several hundred yards from the Cape May Point Lighthouse. (Photo by Charles J. Adams III)

Lake Lily, in West Cape May, where it is said pirates and British warship crews once filled their casks with fresh water. (Photo by Charles J. Adams III)

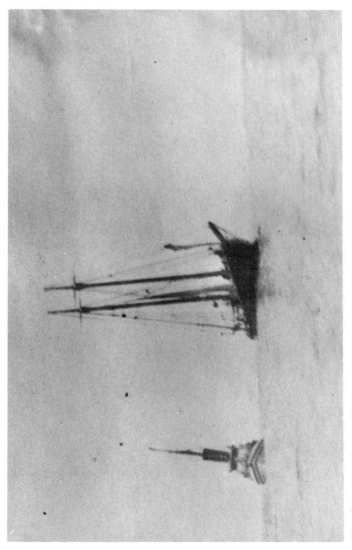

The Coast Guard cutter Kickapoo (left) lays alongside a schooner laden with liquor from Lunenburg, Nova Scotia. The schooner, "Selma Creaser," was just beyond the 12-mile limit, so the Coast Guards could not board her. (Photo courtesy of Ralph Clayton Sr.)

During Prohibition, Coast Guard picket boats like this patrolled the New Jersey shore. This particular craft, based at Ocean City, was armed with a Lewis machine gun and four Springfield rifles. (Photo courtesy of Ralph Clayton Sr.)

This shanty was a typical drop-off point near Cape May raided by Coast Guardsmen during Prohibition. Rumrunners brought their illegal liquor into the bays, up the rivers and to transfer points. The Coast Guard kept a close watch on the practice, and seized much of the bootleg booze. (Photo courtesy of Ralph Clayton Sr.)

Personnel from the Ocean City Coast Guard station, circa 1925, surround a captured rumrunners' truck. From left: Lou Graham, William Henderson, Francis Gifford, Henry Gaskill and Ralph Clayton Sr. (Photo courtesy of Ralph Clayton Sr.)